To Ricky:

I've been meaning book for a wl regalar ya mis libros porque se siente raro, pero para quien me conoce, sabe el valor que pongo en ellas. So consider this an exception and me offering a token of thanks for the friendship and positive vibes. Un fuerte abrazo, kid.

JD

Peace, Love, and Maki Rolls

A Guide to Creative Kindness

By: JD Estrada

Version 1.0

To my mother, I write using your name because
I will always do everything I can to show the world
the strength of our spirit.

To all the Humans 4 Humans that believe and practice the
power of Thoughts & Action.

And to my home of Puerto Rico, this one's for you.

#Humans4PuertoRico

Index

Foreword

Chapter 1:   Emotional Alchemy

Chapter 2:   Creative Kindness

Chapter 3:   There are no problems, only situations

Chapter 4:   Learn more by judging less

Chapter 5:   The healing power of food

Chapter 6:   Explore your inner topography

Chapter 7:   Find your faith

Chapter 8:   Cultivate your fields of knowledge

Chapter 9:   Thoughts & actions

Chapter 10: Listen instead of just waiting for your turn

Chapter 11: Teamwork teaches creative kindness

Chapter 12: Own your faults while rising above them

Chapter 13: Do good, damn it

Chapter 14: Don't waste creativity on excuses

Chapter 15: Manners can change the world

Chapter 16: Define yourself

Afterword

About the Author

Acknowledgments

Humans 4 Humans

Foreword

This particular project is something that's been bouncing around my head for years. It's something I wanted to write but wasn't exactly sure what I wanted it to be on or what would be my motivation.

For years, I've closed blog posts and more recently BookTube videos with the phrase *Peace, Love, and Maki Rolls*. It's just something I said one time and it felt right. It's what I wish upon people which includes peace of mind, love, and of course, good food. I believe when it comes to food, it isn't only an essential part of living but one of the best ways to come together with other like-minded people. In short, one of the best ingredients in life shall be to share food with the best company.

This book comes a decent amount of time after I made a life decision to make as much of a positive impact as I can in the world, be it where I live or work, or in regards to the people I come in contact with throughout the world thanks to the magic of words, small talk, and social media.

It's a peculiar project for several reasons. For starters, the catalyst to write this work came in the form of Hurricane María ravaging my home of Puerto Rico after countless other hurricanes wreaked havoc on Florida, Texas, and the Caribbean in general. It's been an intense process to cope with what's happened and what is happening. In short, I don't think I've ever cried as much as I did during 2017. The thing is that grief, anger, frustration, and all those negative feelings are in essence energy... and I want to use that energy for good.

Within us is the power to choose to do good. To use whatever resources we have to make a difference. So along came the idea for this book to create a *Guide to Creative Kindness* in the hopes of inspiring at least one person to do good.

In regards to genre, it's hard to pinpoint where this book would land in. That's not a problem though since I've never been a fan of labels. So if you find a good category to put it in, by all means let me know. For now, I'll focus on writing and using what is in me to make as positive an impact as I can.

My thanks for coming along for the journey, and of course:

Peace, love, and maki rolls.

JD

Chapter 1:
Emotional Alchemy

Regardless of what you may be feeling at any given moment, you are in control of how you live; even if you feel completely out of control at times.

As humans, we are subject to feelings and emotions among countless other things that help define what we know as humanity. How we live often feels as if it's not up to us but up to intangible forces like fate and destiny.

The curious detail is that at all times there is one factor that is within our grasp and can allow us to be more in control of the trajectory of our lives: a little thing we like to call *choice*. Emotional Alchemy is a term we can use to describe the creative process of taking control over what we feel, taking whatever good or bad we experience and using it to our advantage. To best understand this concept, it is necessary to start by looking at the root words that make up this term.

1. **Alchemy**: (n.) any magical power or process of transmuting a common substance, usually of little value, into a substance of great value.

2. **Emotion**: (n.) any strong agitation of the feelings actuated by experiencing love, hate, fear, etc., and usually accompanied by certain physiological changes, such as increased heartbeat or respiration, and often accompanied by an overt manifestation, such as crying or shaking.

3. **Emotional Alchemy**: (n.) The skill of recognizing emotions as manifestations of energy that we can use

in positive and productive ways to create and make a positive impact.

Feeling powerless is something that happens at certain times in our life where grief gives us a powerful blow that we're not even sure we can recover from. Anger, frustration, sadness, torment, anguish... all these feelings and plenty more can pile on even to the point of rendering you incapable of giving your best. Sometimes it is so intense that it makes even the most basic functions in life seem like a challenge.

But all those emotions we feel can be seen as energy. If you look at these feelings as fuel, you can use them as drivers to do things you might have thought were impossible at one point in your life.

Art is the expression of what we feel in new and creative ways and emotional alchemy can work equally as fuel or inspiration, which aren't the same thing. To better understand how you can use emotions as fuel, take something as common and basic as *anger*. When we don't channel anger effectively, this can lead to stress, which can then lead to a variety of physical maladies. Stress induced anger can be powerful enough to give you a muscle spasm, indigestion, or if intense enough, even cause a heart attack. Imagine how much energy that takes. Now imagine using that energy to do something productive.

If you're angry at something, imagine using that same anger and frustration to do something with it. Imagine if you used that same *destructive* energy to *create*. How many people could you help? How much progress could you make in regards to your projects and goals?

For a real life example, look at the Canadian rock band Rush. After three albums, the band was going through financial problems, had just released an album to lackluster reviews, and were about to be dropped by their record label. Fueled by all this anger and frustration, they created *2112*, one of the seminal albums in prog-rock and honestly a musical journey that leaves fans wanting more at the same time that other musicians are left in the dust in terms of raw musicianship. Where some people would consider tapping out and calling it a day, Rush took to heart their lack of success and created a masterpiece.

If you think that's just one example, it's pretty easy to find plenty more. COUNTLESS people who were considered failures had to persist to succeed. Artists like Bruno Mars and Eminem were on the verge of quitting but persisted, finding their inspiration and motivation to keep going until they had their breakthrough. These are impressive on their own, but imagine a world without the Beatles or Elvis. Both had to dig deep and find something within to create something that would prove naysayers wrong. Walt Disney was told he wasn't creative enough, Oprah Winfrey was shown the door, and examples abound and are easily findable of icons who at one time or another were faced with a choice, quit or push through. Some of these stories are about perseverance, but many are about finding that one true voice and channeling all that energy to break through. It takes energy to keep pushing, to stay perseverant, to see the goal and say that you'll do whatever it takes to make it.

Failure is often shied away from. In fact, we are trained and focused early on to avoid failure at all costs. After all, who likes to fail? It's a type of pain and pretty early on we learn to avoid pain and seek pleasure. But this chapter isn't about success, it's about using what we're dealt with in life and treating the reactions within as energy to create or to fuel.

Some of the most beautiful songs, poems, stories, and movies we come across in our lives are born from heartbreak. That's emotional alchemy. You take something that hurts your very core and you create or more so transfigure those emotions into verse, film, music, or a narrative.

For a personal perspective, I have to say that art is often a matter of using what I feel and what I've lived to create something new. At the end of 2015, I was not at a good point in my life. I was physically breaking and emotionally barely keeping it together. For years, I'd faced whatever challenges life had offered as best as I could, but I kept bottling and putting on a brave face, and taking on more weight until there was a break of sorts. Apart from helping myself with as many resources I had available, I resorted to the act of creating to channel all that pain and frustration and vulnerability in my work. The result was the completion of my second novel, *Shadow of a Human*, and the creation of the longest poem I've written as of yet, *The Madness of Jonathan J. George* (which appears in *Roulette of Rhymes*). I tapped into all I felt to create art from broken emotional shards and this process was essential to my healing.

That's the first time I was truly able to see emotions and pain as energy. I'd used anger before to get into the lineup while surfing or do an extra rep while exercising, but diving that deep into raw emotion to fuel my art was new territory and I was able to see how healing it was.

But it doesn't have to be something that extreme. We all have bad days and I once learned that the best way to improve a bad day is to help someone else. If you're frustrated over something, write someone to tell them you miss them, buy someone a cup of coffee, get a homeless person a meal, or go to a reputable website and make a donation. The intention with this is that even if you're having a bad day, you can do good and that those bad feelings and negative emotions can serve as inspiration to do good in the world, be it a small gesture or a large one.

Return of Investment:

Although plenty of reasons have been given as to why it'd be a good idea to practice emotional alchemy, let's offer a couple of reasons why it's worth your time to practice emotional alchemy.

1. **HEALTH**:

First and foremost, we should reiterate that health is one of the main reasons why practicing emotional alchemy is a good idea. Would you rather have high blood pressure or do something that would help you channel that energy and do something productive? If you verify reputable psychological organizations or if you watch the news with any type of regularity, you will see that more people suffer from anxiety, high levels of stress, and depression than ever before.

To make matters more worrisome, any of these conditions lead to a variety of illnesses from high blood pressure to a higher predisposition to cancer. But don't just look at the facts, think about how you feel when you go through long periods of stress, sadness, or anger. When you view emotions as energy, you can see that if not used, pent up energy can either corrode or become volatile.

If instead you use that energy, then you have a better chance of dealing with situations in a way where you can stay healthy, productive, and driven.

2. **PRODUCTIVITY**:

Using what you feel as a driver means that rather than stay idle, you put that energy to good use. You have a project you haven't finished in months or years? Use that energy to attack that project. Firstly, you'll finally have done what you'd been setting to the side for years. Secondly, you'll look for the next project to finish, which seems to be a much better option to wallowing.

3. **POSITIVE RELATIONSHIPS**:

Imagine if every time you've felt frustrated you did a kind gesture. In the best of days, you can be kind and when you have an off day, you can be even kinder and that goes a long way into being someone people want to be around.

4. **FEELING OF CONTROL**:

One of the main problems of sadness, anger, frustration, and pretty much any negative feelings is that you feel out of control. If instead you consciously and intentionally focus your energy to do something good, that puts **you** in the driver seat. Sure, fate and destiny may have a say, but you are still master of your vessel and you choose how to brave the seas of life.

SUMMARY AND TIPS:

In essence, emotional alchemy is a fancy term that is meant to make it easier for you to be more emotionally in control, simply by changing perspectives. When it comes to our lives, we don't always have control over what challenges we face, but even in the worst of circumstances, we have a choice when we talk about *how* we react and respond to what we experience.

When you're angry, sad, or joyous, you feel that energy within you. If you're in control of how you use that energy, that goes a LONG way towards helping you develop coping mechanisms that can yield some amazing results. And it's all within you.

If you feel sad, do a positive thing to help someone else. If you feel angry or depressed, create something. It's intensely healing not just to create art, but to share it and have someone resonate with the magic you captured. You don't need to be a virtuoso; you just need to be honest about who you are. If you do this, you'll be in control more often and you'll see how things that used to seem impossible, are suddenly attainable, a bit like magic and a lot like alchemy.

Chapter 2:
Creative Kindness

People quite often limit the scope of creativity to the arts when in reality every trade and aspect of our lives can benefit from applying a creative perspective. It takes knowledge and skill to make a building but the vision to make one in the first place was based on creativity. Think about it; at some point, someone got tired of living in a cave and said: "I want a house." Afterwards, they had to decipher how to build it, which brings a whole other aspect of creativity.

It's true to say that engineering requires applied knowledge, but the development of thc fundamentals of every science takes creative vision. A scientist sees a problem and has to get creative in regards to how they will find the solution to said problem. In sports, although players rehearse plays and can run them in their sleep, when they're on the field facing the opposition, improvising and being creative is often the difference between winning and losing.

That we limit the scope and reach of creativity is something that we can remedy every day. As the title of this book suggests, creative kindness can go a long way to changing the world. All we need to do is let loose our creativity and apply it to where and when we can.

On any given day you can be kind and you don't have to do something massive or elaborate, it can be a small detail just to brighten up someone's day. And with today's technological advancements, there's no limit to what you can do.

As a copywriter in several industries, finding creative solutions to communication challenges is my bread and butter, but I do not limit myself to being creative in my work (and this isn't in reference to my path as an indie author). Online, I have profiles on several social media platforms, including Twitter, Google+, Instagram, my blog, Facebook, and YouTube. My approach to each is very different even if there are a couple of things that I do share on more than one platform because I think people in different audiences can enjoy it or get something from what I create.

My approach to each platform has been a learning process throughout the years until I finally learned how I feel comfortable on each, all while doing my best to have a positive impact. That's something that's been a constant with all the efforts, trying to figure out how I can either help someone, write or post something that resonates, or merely sharing something that can put a smile on someone's face.

But it's not just about my *social media presence*. Every day I try to do an act of kindness for loved ones, friends, known people, and strangers alike. This approach came about because once upon a time, I was a cynical and sarcastic guy. Truth be told, I still indulge in sarcasm but there is less bitterness in my approach to life and a whole lot more cheek, because it makes it easier not only to have a positive impact but to be happy in general.

For some examples, I can share a bit of what I do online in my platforms according to the day of the week:

Mondays: On this day I do *Visual Typos* (#VisualTypos) where I take common words or phrases and insert a typo to later create a silly visual. One example has me using the term *Scary Muensters* and instead of a normal werewolf, vampire, or Frankenstein monster, I take three blocks of muenster cheese and put scary things on them to create something cheeky. I don't monetize these and my reasoning is that Mondays are a tough day because it's when we start the week and some cheek and silliness could go a long way to help people smile and apparently it often does.

Tuesdays: For this day, I do two things, *Teactionary* (#Teactionary) posts and *Tasty Tuesdays*. For *Teactionary* entries, I take normal words and spell them incorrectly to integrate the word *tea* in it (Ex. uni-tea, conformi-tea, etc.). This is also cheeky but purely textual in comparison to the visual typos, which are, ahem, visual (hooray for repeating myself). On *Tasty Tuesdays*, I subject myself to recording taste test videos as I try random things for the entertainment of people. Oftentimes I can make a recommendation but every once in a while, I come across something that is plain awful and people apparently crack up at my Jim Carrey facial reactions at whatever I dare to try for the first time. Again, I don't monetize these, I don't get endorsements; it's just me doing something silly to cheer people up. (The most I've gotten was free gum, and hey, who doesn't like free gum?)

Wednesdays: I also go for introspection and I use good ole hump day to do my *SkyThoughts* (#SkyThoughts).

Throughout the year, I take different pictures of the sky and clouds and every Wednesday morning, I write something inspired by that visual. Whatever comes, the idea and intention of this series is to help me get to a better headspace and share that with other people, because you never know who might need to read something positive.

Thursdays: This is a very popular day for people especially on Twitter because it is when I do *Sock it to Me* (#SockItToMe) with the *Sock Family* (#SockFamily). I have an enthusiastic love for quirky socks. This began in part as a response to friends posting boot pictures and as a small personal rebellion in an older job where I had to dress very moderately. That turned into *Sock It To Me*, where I tag a bunch of people and take pictures of my quirky socks, collectibles, mugs, t-shirts, or anything silly just to give people something fun to look forward to on Thursdays. I sometimes accompany this with questions to get people thinking on silly things and just letting loose a bit. By the way, you should know that the *Sock Family* is an <u>inclusive family</u>, where the only rule is to have fun. People don't need to show off their socks, but it is most certainly encouraged.

Fridays: This is another very popular day and all down to me taking daftness as far as I can with *00 Bananas* (#00Bananas). "What the heck is that?" you may ask. Basically I record videos where I play a secret agent that uses a banana instead of a gun as my weapon of choice. All videos last under a minute and are as random as they are silly. But a lot of people seem to enjoy them and my nephews' enthusiasm does nothing to deter me from being a jackass.

In addition to this, I also do *Left Hand Thoughts* (#LeftHandThoughts), which is me writing with my non-dominant hand. Using a pen and a notebook dedicated to this project, I pen messages as encouragement to myself and other people. There's no set day for this, or all the other variety of things I do, but the intention is the same, to cause a smile, maybe inspire a thought, to share something that can resonate, and do my best to make a positive impact while promoting AND practicing creativity.

But this is not just my social media platform mission statement, I leave post-its on desks of coworkers, write friends out of the blue, call or text people, buy a homeless person a lunch and ask them their name to wish them well using their name, and a variety of other things. That's because if you look at your day objectively, you have DOZENS of opportunities to make a positive impact.

I ask and make small talk with security guards and maintenance personnel. I do this so they know I recognize them as fellow humans and that I appreciate all they do for us. On several occasions, I've gotten a security guard a cup of coffee when it's late or candy or a snack or even spotted them lunch. It's a small gesture with big impact and I honestly believe it brings people closer together. It's all about caring and there is a *lot* of power in caring.

Some people limit themselves because they say that the same is not extended back. I can get that sentiment, but I don't let that limit or define me. Within me is the desire to have a positive impact, whether it's recognized and reciprocated or not. And hey, sometimes it *does* go unnoticed or unappreciated. That stings, but we have the choice to keep doing good or find reasons to stop giving our best. The reality is that the things I do bring me joy because it brings joy to other people or allows me to be of use when someone else has been in need.

More examples of things you could do would be as basic as helping with household chores without having to be told, getting someone their favorite candy, spotting someone lunch, or calling them and asking if they want something from the coffee shop.

Even as a kid, I smiled to people on the street, no matter their age, gender, or race. I still do the same and it's my small way of acknowledging their presence and I've also learned that smiles can be occasionally contagious, even if some people don't always smile back and a lot don't even say good morning. Still, I could get all salty at that or I can continue to focus on having done my part to spread the cheer. Again, as mentioned in Chapter 1, we all have that choice and we all have a LOT more choice than we recognize. It's all about being creative and putting your best face on without forcing it.

That's a clarification that needs to be done. Phony stinks a mile away but true cheer reverberates half the world away. When you are kind, make it genuine and the impact you see will be apparent. People will be happy to see you.

This is something that wasn't always the case with me. I used to focus on being a snarky bastard and getting chuckles from people by approaching life like a stand-up skit. True, I got laughs, but it was based on bitching and cynicism... and eventually someone called me out on that. It wasn't the nicest message to receive, but it was a pivotal moment in my life.

Once upon a time, someone whom I was very fond of told me they couldn't keep chatting with me because I always brought them down. That's a hell of a message to give a 19-year-old who swears he knows everything (most of us did think ourselves all-knowing at one point around that age), but that's what I got. Obviously the rift was there and that friendship was never the same, but out of a negative came a positive. I listened to what was told to me and although it took several years to make a true attitude shift, I was eventually able to do that.

Another important detail to mention is that creative kindness is also about spur-of-the-moment decisions and actions. If you see someone who looks like they need help, offer to help. You'll be surprised at how surprised the person will be that you took enough time to look up from your phone to care, connect, and actually help someone. Although that may sound like a snarky comment, that doesn't mean it isn't true.

Kindness can be a small chat away. It can be staring you in the face but if you're disconnected (or more so connected elsewhere), odds are you can miss out on several of those opportunities. But that's OK, online you can make a positive impact in the lives of people a world away and that's also powerful. But trust me, it's important to also be kind in your immediate surroundings for several reasons although a main one is that it enriches your life.

How so? Well think about it; to be kind to someone you HAVE to engage with them. Sure you can leave a random book for someone to pick up, a post-it without making physical contact, but plenty of the opportunities for kindness come from the people you interact with. Think of it this way, kindness is like holding open the door for someone. I hold the door open for men, women, children, grandfathers, mothers with a baby carriage, people with groceries, etc. It's not something I do to allow someone to pass in front of me to check them out. People who do that aren't being kind, they're being opportunistic and you should know how to differentiate between the two.

Being kind is not just one thing, it's a million things and it can be a million more. It all comes down to how creative you allow yourself to be in your life.

Return of Investment:
Creative kindness has countless benefits and more often than not, it will make an impact that will not be limited to your random act of kindness. Still, to illustrate this even more clearly, here are 4 reasons why it's a good idea to invest in Creative Kindness.

1. IT MAKES YOU MEMORABLE

I'm not saying it'll always get the best results, but when you surprise someone with an act of Creative Kindness, they'll remember it for a long time. As a kid, I used to make off-color jokes to a classmate. It's been over 30 years and she still remembers. And damn, being memorable sounds pretty awesome, so why not go for it?

2. YOU WILL NEVER GET BORED

By practicing Creative Kindness, you are consistently looking for opportunities to do something cool for someone you care about or for someone who needs a smile.

3. PEOPLE WANT TO BE AROUND YOU

A lot of people struggle with things in life because let's face it, life isn't exactly easy. But if you often have a good attitude and you want to improve your immediate surroundings, how do you think people will feel about you? I'm not saying it'll always be rosy but it's always better to be received with a smile than eye rolls or a sigh.

4. YOU LEARN TO NOT EXPECT ANYTHING IN RETURN

You won't always get a reaction and that's fine. You're not doing this for the payout, you're doing it for the journey, for the adventure, for the thrill of brightening someone's day. Does that sound sappy enough to be in a Hallmark card? Maybe. But is that really such a bad thing?

SUMMARY AND TIPS:

Creative Kindness is basically being kind in new and creative ways and looking for ways to make yourself and others smile. Creativity need not be limited to the arts but all aspects of your life because it will benefit it in new and amazing ways on a daily basis.

There are no limits except the ones you put on yourself and to be honest, quite often engaging in random acts of kindness is a great way to break a funk we may be going through. It's also a nice way of giving your best while not expecting anything in return and that is a daily lesson because it reminds you to do things because it's what you want to do and not because you will get X or Y payout. The reward should not be the sole thing that defines your path because if that's the case, then you forget to enjoy the journey. Creative Kindness takes every day and says, "OK, what slice of random can we do today to make someone smile?" The best part is that quite often you get great answers and again, it keeps you interested and engaged and there's never a dull moment.

I shared what I do online and in real life to show that there's truly no limit to what you can do if you're stubborn enough to be kind every day. A lot of people need a smile any given day. A lot of people live around you (even in small towns). Imagine the impact you can have if you look at that person and care enough to do something that could make them smile? How to do that? Well that's where you get creative.

Chapter 3:
There are no problems
only situations

There are no problems, only situations.

Rather than take this as a fact, instead use it as a mantra, something you repeat to yourself when things get tough and when inevitably problems *do* come your way. It's quite likely you're thinking this chapter is off to quite the contradictory start and I don't blame you. At face level, it does look as if one statement says the opposite of the other. But let's take a closer look, shall we?

The truth of the matter is that we live in stress-filled and problem-centered times. Anxiety is as prevalent as it's ever been in the world and thanks to news outlets thriving by selling tragedies and bad news, it's pretty easy to fall into a negative streak. If you want proof of this, turn on the news and watch for a full hour. While you do this, take a blank piece of paper, put two columns on said piece of paper, then mark one **Positive** and the other **Negative**. While you watch, put down a news story in one of those two columns but you <u>have</u> to choose one. Why? Because the news should be objective, but it isn't. It's opinionated and for reasons beyond our comprehension, it is highly negative. Naturally, it is quite possible that this spills over into your reality.

Now let's repeat that mantra in the first sentence we saw a couple of lines above: *there are no problems, only situations*. If you look at things objectively, are there problems or situations? By taking out the emotional aspect of problems, you see that they in fact are situations. How they affect you is what turns them into problems and what takes them from an objective position and shifts them into a personal one, more easily skewed to a positive or negative thing.

The term **problem** is defined as *"any question or matter involving doubt, uncertainty, or difficulty."* By the contrary, among the definitions for the word **situation**, you can find it explained as *"a state of affairs; combination of circumstances."* Just by looking at these definitions, which do you think is easier to find a solution for? By the way, this isn't to say that you should be detached or impersonal with the situations that happen to you. What is being suggested is that (sometimes) taking a more objective standpoint can make solutions clearer to you.

For a very common example, think about those times when you can't find your glasses or your keys and you're looking around like a mad person trying to find the thing you're so desperately searching for only to realize that the glasses are on top of your head or the keys are in your pocket or even worse, in your hand. What normally follows can most closely be described as embarrassment because the solution was so close or easy to find that you feel borderline idiotic that you didn't see it. The same goes for many aspects in life.

Most of us have that friend or at the very least know someone who is that type of person who sees a problem or an obstacle in *everything*. These people can actually be invaluable because at one time or another, we need a devil's advocate to find all the chinks in the armor and potential for problems. But it's quite possible that sometimes you'd wish for them to be a bit more relaxed since they always seem stressed and as if happiness has an easy way of eluding them. We can easily call these people pessimistic and they can counter by saying that they are actually behaving like realists and are expecting the worst so that whatever comes their way, they're on the winning side.

This sounds like sound logic and a practical way to live, but it isn't. I know this firsthand because for the longest time I was a pessimist and still fight on a daily basis against having negative thoughts and expecting the worst. Every day I have to work at being an optimist while still being prepared for whatever life throws at me. People say that such an attitude is at odds with the stated behavior, but the reality is that they are not. It's all about being positive without being reckless and choosing to be positive rather than allowing yourself to be swept up by negativity.

There are countless books on the laws of attraction and self-help books like *"The Secret"* that preach things that aren't what I'm referring to. Visualizing good things happening is always... well a good thing, but what is preached quite often remains in the realm of thought or theory. The reality is that you need action to get things done, have progress, and not only wish for but seek and *find* happiness. Thoughts, prayers, visualization, and wishful thinking are nice, yet they rarely get the job done. But we can talk about that further on. For now, let's focus on *situations* being easier to deal with than *problems*.

Knowing when to take an emotional step towards or away

from a situation can help you make better decisions. Is that saying that sometimes you have to get even closer? Why, yes. Empathy is a powerful thing and sometimes a person needs to know you're there, near their shoes, if not standing in them, and doing your best to understand.

Going back to creative kindness, empathy can be seen as a type of emotional role-playing where you do your best to offer a solution to someone you care about or heck, even yourself. Call it advice through method acting if such a fancy title makes sense to you. Now you may ask yourself, does this contradict the approach of seeing things as situations rather than problems? The short answer is no.

The question to ask now would be why it doesn't, which can be countered by another question: if you get emotionally involved with something, does it have to immediately become a problem or make the situation endlessly harder to solve? The point being made is to show that we can engage emotionally with situations without being swept in a wave of worry, cynicism, gloom, or whatever negative thing you can think of. If this is so, then why can't we do the same for ourselves? Why can't we have less problems and more solvable situations?

When you boil most things down, if it's a problem or not comes down to the connotation and context we give the situation. The reality is that sometimes we can be fully in control and sometimes due to emotional involvement, the options we have or don't have, or because of a basic lack of information, we are less in control than we'd ideally like to be. So let's look at each of these separately and see what options we have.

Emotional involvement:

Many problems we have are problems because either we're involved, someone we know is involved, or because it's something very important to us. As mentioned above, emotional involvement can actually be a good thing, but quite often it can cloud judgment or reduce our overall vision of a situation. It's not to say you should be a robot. It's saying that recognizing how emotions affect us can help us manage things better.

Amount of options:

Solutions come from choosing an option to respond to any given situation based on how we think said option would help us handle whatever we are facing. Many problems we have often come down to feeling as if we have either limited options or none at all, or at the very least, not feeling too enthusiastic with the options we have available. By looking at the situation as objectively as possible we can see the options we have and we can see if these options are enough or if we need more. If we need more, that's where creativity comes in and quite often, there's at least one more option which initially wasn't obvious to you. Focus on that, on getting one more option. If you have an overabundance of options, say 10, put them down on a paper and take off the obvious ones that aren't the best fit for the situation for whatever reason. Sometimes in this process, one option kind of stands out, but if not, at the very least it's easier to pick from 7 than it is from 10. Do the process again until you get to a few options where each can offer you a manageable outcome. A simple situation is deciding where to eat. If you have 10 options, you might be overwhelmed and end up not deciding on anything. Use any means to knock a couple of options down. Don't want Mexican? Tired of pizza? Not hungry enough for steak? Curious about some vegan options? Ask all those questions and help yourself out. Also, regardless of what you're facing, think of the situation as a test; right now you just the need the answers that will help you "pass the test", it doesn't need to be the perfect answer and you don't need to get 100 in the test. You just need to pass. If the options you have aren't to your liking, then ask yourself, what is it that you don't like? Take your list, cross off something and as much as you can, put the why you've crossed out that option. What makes them unpleasant? Will you have to pass unnecessary hardship? Or is it that the situation is in general unpleasant? Some things in life aren't a joy to handle, but you have to handle them. Use the same process as above and look for the option that offers you the least unpleasant option but that will offer a solution. Too often we choose something that allows us to conform or tolerate and all this does is prolong the situation while offering the illusion of solution. It's also worth noting, sometimes the unpleasant option is the right one. So to help you arrive at your decision, it could definitely help if you focus on what the best option is, even if it is unpleasant. Whatever you do, don't fool yourself or else it'll be worse in the long run.

Lack of information:

Not knowing what's going on or not knowing information you think is vital is a very common problem. For instance, a few years back, my mother was acting weird, she was cryptic yet obviously something was very wrong but she couldn't tell me. It wasn't until I spoke to my brother that he told me my mother had been diagnosed with breast cancer. For those several hours before I knew what was wrong, I was lost, frustrated, scared, and angry, because I knew something was wrong and something serious. As soon as I knew what it was, I actually calmed down, because knowing meant that we had options, that we could put a name to the situation and that it could be solved. Although this journey was all on mom, the support we offered helped in some way. She didn't want to tell me because it would upset me, but in the end, knowing exactly what she was facing was the best way for all of us to face the same situation and use all our resources and attack it head on. This is actually very common. We don't want to burden people or we fear the reaction of people to the situation we have to face. Although most of us can appreciate this, the fact remains that when there is information shared, solutions can be found. And if someone flakes out because they can't handle it, then that is something to address later. Not all situations will be this dire, some might even be direr, but the fact remains, when you need the support of others, you need a team that is in it to win it and who works together.

Return of investment:

When you treat life events like situations rather than problems, that helps you be more in control of what is happening and how you will handle the situation. There is no guarantee of success because in life there are very rare instances where there is any sort of guarantee. Creative kindness enters the picture when you practice empathy, when you don't judge and focus on listening, when you look at options objectively and find the information you need. The benefits of using it are as varied as the possible outcomes.

1. CONTROL BRINGS CLARITY

Emotions can be a powerful thing but so can control. In situations of extreme duress, emotions can spike adrenaline and allow you to do superhuman things. They can also make the clearest solutions all but impossible to see.

2. YOU BECOME BETTER AT GRADING OPTIONS

Knowing what you can do is almost as good as knowing which are the best options. By taking a more objective view, you realize that you're not aiming for perfection, but for the best possible solution, and that means there's a margin of error. In short, it's accepting that there's no one answer to situations and that as long as a solution serves its purpose, you can put that in the win column.

3. KNOW THYSELF AND YOU'LL KNOW THY SOLUTIONS

None of us are perfect and in life, we're just doing our best to be our best. That means knowing what our faults are and looking to negate them as much as possible.

SUMMARY AND TIPS:

By no means am I preaching that I know the solution to every situation, but I do know that I do my best to offer the best solutions I can. This includes a lot of listening, empathy, role playing, and getting creative to find information, options, or help.

I know what some of my weaknesses are. For me, not having the facts works to my disadvantage, so I know I need to learn vital information before I can give the best answers. For other people, it's time, so they would have to decipher how to buy themselves time to think more clearly. For others, emotions can interfere so maybe they need a minute to cool down, so for them learning breathing exercises could be the difference between a solution and exacerbating a situation.

It all boils down to knowing who and how you are and what you can offer in life. If you have too many options, visualize them as best as you can to eliminate and simplify. Do a rough go to cut down to size and refine what you use to differentiate each round until you get the best solution.

Also, make sure to write down your situation so you can visualize it and hold it in your hand. Suddenly it's tangible even at an unconscious level and quite often defining a situation can offer the solution quicker. And if all else fails, remember how we started this chapter and repeat after me:

There are no problems, only situations.

Chapter 4: Learn more by judging less

The less you judge the more you learn.

If you take anything at all from this book, I honestly hope this line makes the cut, honestly. You see, prejudice is not only the great divider, it is the great blinder, the loud deafening distraction, and the endless limiter. It closes you off to learning as much as you can, and for what? A set of supposed beliefs?

Religion, politics, gender, sports, music, psychology, food, friendship, and beyond. The more you explore and try to learn, the richer your life will be because information and experience always allow you to broaden your perspective. The problem comes when you don't want to hear what someone else has to say or try to understand their perspective. Truth be told, some topics and some situations will put your values to the test and there will come an impasse. However, it's very different to allow a person their opinion than needing to win the argument, especially when and where there isn't any.

Take any of the topics mentioned at the beginning of the last paragraph and you will find groups that are in conflict. You may ask, but how can food or friendship be a motive for conflict? Simple, take a group of friends and try to decide who are the best friends or who is the best friend, meaning the one who's always been there. Let's face it, in some contexts, such a discussion can turn ugly and fast. As for food, there's nothing like people debating which culinary tradition is the best. Quite simply, it's easy to create conflict with the mere requirement of being inflexible in your opinion or being eager to judge.

I'm extremely fortunate that people ask me for advice on occasion or come to me to talk about some situation or another. I shall always do my best to listen, because it's not my job to judge, but to listen and do my best to help.

One fond example I can give came while I was waiting in line for coffee. I bumped into a friend while waiting in the queue. It was very nice to see her and I always remembered how nice she was and how often she invited me to her Bible group and several Christian activities. I always thanked her for the invitation but told her that although I had grown up Catholic, I had opted to be agnostic and although I appreciated the offer, I wasn't sure I was a good fit because I just wasn't into it. Regardless, I thanked her every single time and meant it.

So we're there in the queue and she tells me she wants to study theology but wasn't sure. My reaction? I thought that was a perfect fit. She had always shown that she cared about it and I could remember her enthusiasm on this topic so I told her that I truly believed she could make a great impact in that path. When I finished my little spiel, she had a weird look on her face before getting a bit misty-eyed and thanking me because I was the *first* person to say that it was a good idea. Everyone else she'd told had said she'd go hungry, that it was a stupid career choice, and a waste of time. She told me this and I thought it was unnecessarily harsh, so I couldn't even begin to think what she had felt when she heard that and clearly from several people. I repeated my opinion and told her to follow what *she* thought was best for her and to make it work. People mean well, but they often don't know better than to think their opinion is your reality. She gave me the biggest hug ever and told me she really needed to hear that, which is funny, since I'm agnostic and I was rooting for her to embrace theology. And you know why? Because it wasn't about me or my beliefs or what I would do with my life. It was about *her* journey on *her* path.

A lot of people offer advice based solely on their experience or what they think is best for them without even realizing that is what they are doing. To do so is an injustice to the path of another person which is way different from yours, even if you share opinions on several topics. When you *take the time to understand where someone is coming from*, that is another example of using creative kindness to practice empathy.

The problem comes when someone needs to be right or worse yet, *superior*. Too often, people focus on "winning" in as many ways as you can imagine. Sometimes this is a reaction from how they feel about themselves, but in many people it's basically how they're wired or how they were brought up. They know the *best* restaurants, listen to the best music, follow the best teams, and vote for the best candidates.

For some reason, I'm reminded a little of how law is practiced. It's not about finding justice, it's all about winning, which is why so many people get away with murder, literally. By focusing on a technicality, we set free someone who is clearly guilty and woohoo, money was made and another W for the record. But what about justice? Sad to say, but quite often that's secondary.

For some reason or another, people are highly competitive and crave a win much more than a resolution or any type of compromise, which is odd since there's so much to gain from win-win situations.

The fact remains that the more open you are to learn, the richer your life can be. I may define myself as heterosexual, but I have friends all over the spectrum of sexuality. I honestly think the only gender I don't have some sort of acquaintance is transgender, but I do know people who identify themselves as gay, lesbian, bisexual, asexual, agender, and gender fluid. Every time I come in contact with someone with a new definition, it's an opportunity to learn because what leads each person to their definition is particular to them. Learning to talk with someone who is agender and doesn't like pronouns like she/her/he/him makes it challenging to communicate, but it's an enriching experience because it offers a new perspective. The same with people of any gender and the more people you know, the clearer it becomes that there is no one answer as to why people choose to define themselves one way or another, and that's a beautiful thing. People shun people for being gay or just plain ole "weird" when in reality the only thing that they are is *different*. Fortunately, last I checked, different isn't bad.

The challenge comes when we tackle topics where it's hard to understand the other perspective because it's either so far removed from your own that it's a challenge or simply because the possibility of conflict is so easy. Simply put, some people have no interest in seeing eye to eye with you or seeing things from a different point of view, and although sad, that's something we have to sometimes accept. I know some people whose opinion on topics varies so much from mine that they've taken a step away from me because of our differing opinions, which is odd and more than a little sad. Last I checked, life doesn't work based on mandatory consensus, but unfortunately some people will like you only as long as they can agree with you, which seems like an extremely weird way to live or be happy.

I try to have very strong beliefs but I always do my best to listen to dissenting opinions if only to get another perspective. Sometimes another person's perspective won't make any sense to me, but often there will be something that you can get from a varying opinion. By being open to new opinions and experiences, I've learned a lot and realized how little I know about pretty much everything and how much more I still have to learn.

The lesson being recommended is that of acceptance because if we listen and accept, good things happen. There hasn't been one instance in my life where I have not benefitted from shutting my mouth and listening. Besides, it offers the opportunity to internalize and think of your response.

Alas, too often people shoot from the hip and are quick to judge. I can't begin to imagine all the restaurants and cuisines and dishes I would have missed out on if I didn't allow myself to try something new. How many bands, movies, books, and artists I wouldn't know. Lord knows how many people I wouldn't have made the acquaintance of if I had limited myself.

In reference to that last point, if I would remain immovable in regards to my opinion, I would not have realized that some people who didn't make the best first impression were in fact some amazing humans. If I would cast out people whose views I don't agree with or understand, I'd be left quite alone. Life is meant to be lived and experienced. The more we limit our opportunities to discover it the more we miss out on. So by all means, drop your shields and dive in the deep end to explore new depths. Who knows what wonders you will find.

Return of Investment:

Prejudice is easy to preach against. It honestly goes against the best humanity has to offer. Some people think it's a simpler way to live, but the reality is that it's simply a more limited way of living. Although there are countless reasons to judge less, here are four.

1.   EVERY DAY BRINGS NEW SURPRISES

Prejudice limits what you learn from life and what you can experience. By being open to new experiences you will find opportunities of enrichment at every single corner. From music, to movies, to books, to food, to life in general. The world not only becomes your oyster, it becomes your oyster, your hot dog, your piece of cake, or whatever else you decide to try.

2.   YOU FIND IT HARDER TO FIGHT

When you allow yourself to not judge and instead listen, fighting becomes increasingly harder, simply because your focus switches from *needing to win* to *needing to understand*.

3.   YOU LEARN THE MOST RANDOM THINGS

A lot of people miss out on so much because they don't think they're going to like something... even if they haven't tried it. When you stop judging, you become more open to learning about any and everything and hey, that'll make you the talk of the party, make elevator rides more interesting, and transform you into a full on asset on trivia nights.

4.   YOU SEE MORE HUMANS AND LESS CATEGORIES

We are excellent at segmenting things based on castes, categories, and segments. Maybe it goes to those Darwin tendencies where we need to name and label things. Still, labeling and judging blind you to the full aspect of people. By dropping the judgment, you can see that everyone has several layers and that there are many shades of color in any given person to discover if we only get over ourselves and our need to judge.

SUMMARY AND TIPS:

Judging is almost a sport that most of us partake in. The less we judge the less we feel the need to "win" and the more we crave to learn. Life is a wonderful opportunity to learn and anything that prompts us to learn and experience more is for the betterment of humankind.

Does that mean you can switch off your prejudice? More than that, it means that you can identify when you're having a knee-jerk reaction and keep yourself in check. If you find yourself waiting for your turn to respond rather than listening, this is also a good time to check yourself and before offering your opinion, repeat what the person just said to make sure you understand. After you do that, explain your point of view and then try to find where they converge. This is just one example, but I guarantee that it will avoid a whole lot of conflict in your life and instead offer you opportunities galore to learn.

If you're constantly afraid to try new things, bring up some music streaming service and search in music genres you normally avoid. See if there's something you like and search further. If you've never tried a type of food, try a fusion place that does fusion with a type of cuisine you *do* like to take baby steps to discover new things. Make a couples night or group outing out of trying new things and record your reactions. At the very least you will have a blast, document the adventures, and who knows, maybe a video goes viral.

The main message is for you to see things you don't understand, listen, and learn. Who knows? You might even enjoy it.

Chapter 5: The healing power of food

Breaking bread is a good thing. Scratch that. Breaking bread is an amazing thing.

Although we may differ in countless ways, there are a couple of things that bring us together or that every human needs to do to survive. We all need to breathe, we all go to the bathroom, and we all eat. How we go about engaging in any of these activities can actually vary greatly from one place to another.

If you have asthma and allergies, your breathing is different from a person who does not. If you practice yoga, your way of breathing is probably very different from someone who hasn't been shown proper breathing techniques. But we all breathe. Go to bathrooms in the US, Europe, Asia, or in the great outdoors and you'll see that although we all have to answer nature's call, we don't all answer the same way.

The same goes for food, although this one is the easiest category to see how we differ. Still, it's no surprise that the Caucus Room in Washington DC is famous for being one of the few places where members of both major parties in the country sit down to eat and discuss whatever's on the table, be it politics or great food.

Breaking bread could refer to many things, from the religious (breaking the Eucharist during mass) to a truce offering. The fact remains that food quite often brings us together and can actually help us bridge gaps created by society.

Think about it, can you honestly say that even the most

racist person wouldn't allow themselves to indulge in the delights held within something as simple as a taco? Do you think the most anti-white person wouldn't enjoy a slice of apple pie? Just the thought of it is silly, which is a good point if you want to discuss racism with someone, but I digress. After all, it's quite possible there are people who don't like tacos or apple pie. To each their own, but seriously, are they missing out or what?

The point being made is that food brings us together.

Families come together over the holidays to spend time together and share food. Quite often there's even a full-on ritual, some people say grace, and in some families, whoever gets to carve a turkey is basically the honored guest. Some of the best memories you will have will be tied directly to food. That's in part because food engages so many senses and bonds them to memory. The sense that most ties with memory is smell. There are smells that will take you way back to your kindergarten years, to your grandmother's house, to the beach, and several other places in your life. If you take a wonderful smelling dish and combine it with amazing flavor, a peculiar yet enjoyable texture, and share that meal with someone you care about, odds are extremely high that this memory will definitely stick for a LONG time... and that's a beautiful thing to experience.

But it doesn't stop there, food teaches us about culture. From the ingredients to the way food is prepared and served, culture is in every bite and every dish we prepare.

Spices, meats, vegetables, fruits, and drink vary from one place to another and regardless of the endless debates people can have, there truly isn't a cuisine that's better than the other. It's simply a matter of being different. Some dishes are spicier than others, some focus on texture, and what is amazing is that food that was originally a staple for people of scarce resources, have bridged the gap between classes. Soups offer so many examples. Take a look at cream of potato or French onion soup. These may be fancy dishes in many places nowadays, but this was the food of poor people who had to make do with what they had. And boy did they ever.

Like these, we can find countless examples showing that if food doesn't discriminate, then why should we?

But don't limit yourself to edibles, think of drinkables and how often what we drink brings us closer together. That glass of wine you share with a loved one. That toast of champagne at a wedding. That tea that helped you calm your friend. The sports drink that the team spilled over the coach. That coffee you shared in the AM with a lovely acquaintance. The reason it's so common is because quite often we "don't have time" for a meal but always have time for a drink, and that's actually true. Although it's beyond common for a cup of coffee to turn into a 2-hour conversation, you also have the convenience that if you have to cut it short, you can.

When you also look at the needs we see on a daily basis, feeding your fellow human can also be an immensely healing experience. Someone down on their luck might wonder where they will get their next meal. Now imagine you're the answer to one of those meals. It could be that you bought someone a meal, gave them your leftovers, made a donation to an organization that focuses on feeding the needy, or maybe you even shared your meal by literally taking a piece of bread from your plate and giving it to someone. This single act is so incredibly powerful that it can change a life.

That we don't do it that often is down to either saturation of bad news, indifference, or even fear. But trust me, there have been plenty of times in my life where sharing a meal with someone or sponsoring them a meal has made all the difference in a day, for them as well as for me. Some people might say that if you do it once, you'll have to do it every time. Although I can see the logic of the statement, I don't see why it has to be a bad thing to take off your plate and share with other people. For me, if I see someone in need, the option to help them is on the table and I do my best to take that opportunity often though I could do it much more frequently than I do. Some days I haven't done it for whatever reason I can come up with, valid or not. Those days stick with me for the wrong reasons while the days I ask someone, "do you have something to eat?" and can make sure they're fed for at least that one meal stick with me for the right reason.

What is apparently peculiar is that I ask people what they want. I don't look at the cheapest item on a menu and don't limit their options. On more than one occasion I've been met with confused looks of people who don't know how to react to me asking them what their preference is. Food is food, right? I clarify that they caught me on a good day and that I want to let them pick whatever they want because they shouldn't be limited when it comes to a good action. Does this mean I've bought people meal and dessert? You bet it does.

Here's the thing, offering someone food shouldn't come with restrictions. For me, it's two questions: _do you want to eat_ and _what do you want to eat_. Some people have said that I'm not helping these people out by giving them a handout. Again, although I can see their reasoning and I could find reasons aplenty of why I shouldn't give of my money and food, something inside me insists on giving them food (I'm way warier of giving money away blindly).

Beyond the social setting, food can also heal in a myriad of individual ways. It should be no surprise that the best remedy for a close call with a dementor from the Wizarding World of Harry Potter is to eat chocolate. After all, it's chocolate. Chocolate elevates moods and is good for you in several ways. In excess, it'll throw a protest in your stomach but in moderation (and if you actually enjoy chocolate or aren't allergic) it can actually improve your day drastically.

We all have our favorite foods that transform into comfort foods. It could be ice cream, your mom's rice dish, a cold beer, candy, or even a warm cuppa tea. What doesn't change is that when you've had a particularly rough day, something as simple as food or drink can help you recalibrate and shake off any funks that might have clung on to your clothes.

If you add the medicinal properties of several foods, you can see that there is yet another aspect of healing when it comes to food and drink. Pineapple and papaya have natural anti-inflammatory properties. Cinnamon can help you regulate blood sugar. Soursop and ginger can promote healthy digestion. Like these, you can find countless examples of how good food can be for you. By the same token, some guilty pleasures may be bad for the body, but boy can they make your mood better. It's no secret that cookies and candy aren't that great for you, but sometimes a little sweet goes a long way to remedying sour times. Just remember that magic word, *moderation*. It will make sure you don't overindulge and turn a good thing into a belly ache.

What's fascinating in all of these examples is that quite often food can be more effective than medicine when it comes to remedies. Apart from the placebo effect in regards to countless remedies, which establishes that the psychological aspect of taking a remedy can yield results even if the "medication" is a sugar tablet, a proper diet can go a long way to prolonging, improving, and optimizing life. Beyond what you hear that you should be eating, what's more important is you listening to your body and what it says when you eat or drink something. A lot of people want to follow a list of foods to live forever even if they aren't good for them. Sometimes it comes down to an allergy, but maybe sometimes it's just a small inconvenience, like having to go to the bathroom, feeling tired, feeling agitated, or acid reflux. Some people insist they always need their coffee, even if they have GERD (Gastrointestinal Reflux Disease). I'm not exaggerating.

That we insist we eat and drink things that immediately have consequences and don't have any positives should be a clear sign that we need to modify our behavior. Here's where creativity can be applied in at least two examples: 1. You can be creative in finding alternatives to your coffee or 2. You can be creative in the ways you convince yourself that there are healthier options out there. Are there more options? No doubt there are, like finding natural remedies or foods and practices that can help your body heal. What limits or expands is your need to find solutions or options.

When it comes to creative kindness in food: this can go from something as simple as making someone's favorite dish or finding them remedies for different maladies. Although I know a lot of people with insomnia who have tried everything, some people with milder symptoms have benefitted from information I've shared in regards to natural sleep remedies. Yogurt, almonds, lavender, vanilla, and lettuce water can all help and this is information I've learned from searching for options for people I care about. With other people, physical activity has been the key and I've been able to recommend breathing exercises or shifts in daily routines that can help. What remains constant is the desire to want to help someone out. What changes are the remedies and options I find for one person versus another.

But kindness doesn't have to just be about healing. Want a great idea to make your work environment a bit chipper from time to time? Find out the favorite candy/snack of a co-worker. Don't make it obvious about getting the information and when you do finally get them that little sumthin-sumthin, make sure it comes out of the blue. That you take time to think about someone you work with can go a long way in making for a better work environment or drastically improving someone's day. I know this from experience and it's still something I do from time to time. I make a point not to make it constant because if it becomes routine, it loses that bit of magic, but if you keep it random enough, it tends to pack a bigger punch.

Return of Investment

Food is something that can unite more than it can divide if we give it the chance. It can also heal physically as well as emotionally. Here are four reasons why you should apply creative kindness to all things food related.

1. KNOW A PERSON THROUGH THEIR FAVORITES

Getting to know people is a fascinating process and you can learn a lot about someone from the food they love.

2. GETTING GIFTS GETS EASIER

68

When you know the things someone loves, you can find similar things to help them expand their horizons. Know someone who loves chocolate, try getting chocolate from different countries or exotic truffles. Know someone who loves to cook, gift them some offbeat spices or flavored oils.

3. COST EFFICIENT WAY OF BEING A BETTER HUMAN

You can buy someone a full meal and it'll set you back what, $10? Not a bad investment to be a better human. But hold on, it doesn't even need to be $10. If you spot someone some good coffee (that needn't be from a pricey coffee shop) you can make an act of kindness for less than $2. Heck, you can even ask the cashier to charge you two coffees and to offer one for free to the next person that comes around.

4. YOU CAN TAKE FEWER MEDS

Imagine finding better options for your conditions than a roulette of medications? Sounds like something most of us could and should invest in, not only because it's a more natural option, but because in regards to cost, there is no comparison.

SUMMARY AND TIPS:

Food can heal on a physical, personal, social, and emotional level. It is one of the great unifiers in our life and an easy way to expand your horizons and get to know new cultures. It's also a nice way to connect with people far removed from what you've known up to this point in your life.

Creative kindness can be applied to food in so many ways that the only limit you have is yourself and what your imagination can come up with. Learn about food, share food, and bring people along for the adventure.

Are you afraid of certain dishes? Then what's the worst that can happen, that you don't like it and need to rinse your mouth? Then try something else until you find the weird things that make you smile every time you see them. You might find that you like sea urchin. You might discover that vegan plates can be adventurous and meaty in their meatlessness. You might also discover things that are good for you or maybe even better for you than what you typically eat. Want a trip in time? Try a dish typical from a different era. Again, the possibilities are endless and there's so much enjoyment to be had that limiting yourself seems silly.

So have fun, serve yourself something different, try a new flavor, ask for a bartender or chef to go hog wild based on the things you like and discover pieces of your soul one bite at a time.

Chapter 6: Explore your inner topography

Introspection is meant to be a learning experience, not an easy one.

Mental and emotional health are two main issues millions of people face on a daily basis. I have had issues where I've had to seek assistance and that's something more people should feel comfortable with because if there's anything that's dangerous it's playing the tough guy or gal where your mind is concerned.

Too often people ignore emotions or bottle things inside in the interest of avoiding conflict. It's understandable, no one really wants conflict in their lives, but ignoring issues won't make a situation go away. Quite often, all it will do is aggravate it. But that's just one aspect of introspection, let's call it the obvious one. That there is a mental health situation worldwide should come as no surprise. That people take medications if only to make existence more tolerable shouldn't be a surprise either. That people don't take the time to get to know themselves in the slightest is what really surprises me.

Within each of us there is a vast intricate world begging to be explored. It's there and it is ignored on a daily basis because we're too busy, because we're too overworked, or because maybe we won't like what we see. The fact of the matter is that no one is perfect and we all have areas of opportunity along with aspects of our personality that although intrinsically ours, they're not our favorite parts of who we are.

For me, my temper has never been to my liking even

though it's gotten better. Rather than ignore this, I've done my best to not only work on it, but to genuinely get to know myself. What things set me off? How many of those things are down to how I view life? How many are issues that it's understandable to not like, and how many are more on the lines of being a pet peeve? That I sometimes get easily distracted isn't to my liking either, but I counter that by having bouts of hyper-focus where nothing else exists except the task at hand.

These are all aspects of my personality and things I can get to know better at the same time as I work on them so I'm happy with how I am. That's another thing, people often modify their behavior to suit the needs and likes of other people, which is a recipe for disaster if there ever was one. I modify what I think could change for my benefit, not anyone else's. A lot of people expect others to adjust and conform to what they would find approvable, which is as childish as it is selfish.

Subsequently, we can also take a better look at our physical appearance and how we respond to it. There are industries that thrive on people's insecurities by telling them how they should look, what they should wear, and how you can be successful/attractive/desirable based on how you modify those looks. I'm not saying there is a lack of logic to this, I'm saying that quite often people spend hours upon hours improving things and changing who they are for an audience rather than for their own betterment as an individual.

When it comes to exploring who and how you are, being honest with yourself is the most important thing. This means that you need to honestly say what you like and don't like about yourself and why. In addition to that, getting to know your body is something a lot of people don't take advantage of, which would actually save them a LOT of troubles and aches. Simply put, what's more important, finishing a set at the gym or cutting it short because you're aware of what your body is saying? Now take the gym and replace that setting with your posture, what you eat, what you drink, how many hours you sleep, how often you interact with people, what music are you listening to, what movies are you watching, what are you reading? Each of these things and hundreds more are pieces that make who you are and impact you on a daily basis in regards to how the way you go about experiencing reality.

Getting to know yourself is one of the most fascinating things because how you perceive and interpret what your senses offer you is a unique experience that you can try to explain to someone else but won't be able to. Most of us are blessed with all our senses yet we take them for granted. There's no reason to do so and that's one area where creative kindness can have an impact on your life.

I'm a big fan of listening to a wide variety of music, watching all sorts of movies, trying new and weird foods, and pretty much doing my best to expose myself to new experiences and information if only to further open myself to more things in this trip we call life.

In terms of vision, I love seeing new amazing vistas and have a mild appreciation of art to the point where I can go to a museum and have a wonderful time. It's partially because of how I react to new visual stimuli and it's also because as a writer, anything can inspire an idea for a story or a detail within a story. I've known to take a notebook with me to capture the feelings within in reaction to a river or even a tree. Nature and life itself are fascinating things but it's also fascinating how any and everything can trigger a reaction within. Why does a sunset make me sigh? Why does a falling flower make me cry if it lands face down or smile if it lands on a little stream and floats on off? Why does the color black fascinate me so much? Why do colors that I used to not like suddenly grab my attention? Our eyes are absolutely amazing but the tricks vision plays on us are equally remarkable. Why if we walk past a fence it gets blurry? Why does a straw in a glass look as if it's split wrong?

When you also observe movement, there are even more fascinating things to watch. Take a video where someone tosses a ball and watch it. Now watch it in fast forward. Then watch it in super slow motion. Then watch it in reverse. It's mesmerizing how the same action can be seen in so many ways. In regards to nature, there are certain patterns that are enthralling to watch. Sit on a beach and enjoy the waves breaking towards the shore. Watch for a long while and realize the magic that a wave is because like a snowflake, no two are identical. They may be similar, but never identical. See the patterns in the waves, the place where the wave always breaks, how often the waves come and how winds groom the surface of a wave to make it stand taller if it's offshore or crumble if it's onshore.

Further exploring other senses, if you take the time to really hone in on sound, you'll find even more wonders. For one part, there's something wonderful about differentiating the instruments within a symphony. On the flip side, there's also something amazingly powerful of an artist with their voice and one instrument and nothing else. It's intimate. It's sharing something that stirs something within them and us as well. When you watch horror films, notice how the best horror movies have intricate soundscapes. See how that screeching violin slices across your spine. Feel how that disjointed piano mimics the movement of something that goes bump in the dark. Hear the beat of your heart and see how your breathing plays along with it. Heck, take the time to really listen to your stomach and all the weird noises it does.

As for the sense of smell, it's just as impressive and it's one of the most refined senses we take for granted and one of the ones that can most easily modify how we feel. How so? It's no accident that houses when they're being shown to potential buyers have cookies in the oven. It's also no accident that scents of ginger and lavender are used at spas and during massage therapy. Think about it, can you imagine a toothpaste that doesn't have a minty smell that you're truly sold on? Wine enthusiasts can also tell you the properties of the soil where a wine was grown. Some are accurate while others might simply be indulging in some fancy shmansiness. But that doesn't change that some people have a highly refined sense of smell.

Touch is another peculiar sense because it is the sightless sight. If you have a frame of reference of something and you touch it with your eyes closed, you can reconstruct it in your mind. But have you ever thought about how you feel when you wear that special shirt you love so much? Have you ever laid down on fresh bed sheets only to basically melt in that lush sensation? What about when you shake someone's hand? The rough hands, the soft hands, the warm hands that somehow tell you that this is a friend. Or how about when you hug someone? How committed are you to that hug? How many types of hug do you give? Your sense of touch is activated in so many ways yet we simply focus on the obvious things.

Taste is just as powerful as well. Sometimes you taste something that you immediately fall in love with. With other things, the taste of it shifts so often that your brain works overtime in an attempt to keep up with what it's experiencing. Some tastes are unpleasant, some are great. Some change with time.

Actually, that's the magic of the senses and of getting to know yourself. How you perceive one thing at this point in time may shift in the near or not so near future. The same goes for thoughts and opinions. It's all about experience and learning. That's why sometimes you watch or read or listen to something you don't like only to be surprised a few years down the road on how much you have grown to love it.

When it comes to yourself, creative kindness is best expressed when you take the time to get to know yourself and actually enjoy spending time alone. It's not to say that you should be a lone wolf or anything, but the power of being comfortable with your deepest thoughts goes a long way to deciphering what your definition of happiness is. In addition, a lot of what we do or don't do is for fear of being alone. So imagine what your life would be like if your pursuit of happiness was freed in such a manner.

Life is an amazing experience if you allow it to be. The more you let the real you out, the more things you'll find that fascinate you and that are particular to you. Too often people conform to what is expected from them. Trends and fashions are followed and too often we lose sense of who we are because we decided to follow advice from a magazine column rather than go in the direction pointed by our heart compass.

That's just it though, your gut is smarter than you and it's been demonstrated that parts of your physiology beyond the brain can be as smart, smarter, or at least more intuitive, than the brain. At a cerebral level, we are brilliant at overthinking things but when something *feels* right, you don't need to think anything. You don't have to force anything either. You can just be. But if you constantly distract yourself or numb yourself to the real you, then who do you expect to see in the mirror looking back? What can you expect to feel if you focus on conforming and repressing?

Your inner world is far vaster than you can imagine and you can spend a lifetime searching and documenting within without finding out all there is to you. So stop selling yourself short. Stop missing out on yourself. See the light and the dark. See the beautiful and the damaged. See the real you. And keep searching, for there is no limit to your depths. There is only a limit to how far you're willing to dive.

Return of Investment:

Psychology has had to fight hard to get whatever respect it gets from the medical community, but the implications and impact it can have can be profound. Socrates once said, that "the unexamined life is not worth living," which is why he recommends to "know thyself." Although there are several reasons why this is good for you, here are four.

1. YOU WILL NEVER BE FORCED INTO ANYTHING

When you know who you are and what you stand for, peer pressure ceases to exist. You know the ground on which you walk on and anything you explore is because you choose it, not because of anyone else.

2. YOU WILL LEARN EVERY DAY

There is a world within you waiting to be discovered,

begging for attention so you can learn what it is that truly makes you happy. Your body, your mind, and your soul will continue to be enriched the more you get to know each part of you. Life is the engagement of the senses and there is no end to what you can learn about life and yourself.

3. YOU WILL NEVER GET BORED

When you look at life as an exploration, every day holds new adventures. By realizing this, you see that boredom is actually a choice and not a very good one in regards to how you invest time and energy. Life is all about choice. So imagine how much more fascinating it can be if you choose to be amazed?

4. YOU WILL ALWAYS BE TRUE TO YOU

The better you know who you are, the easier it is to be you. A lot of people spend their lives emulating people they admire, which is a shame. Within them, there is the potential for something unique and memorable. Think about it, would you settle for being the best tribute band in the world, or do you want to be appreciated for being you?

SUMMARY AND TIPS:

Getting to know yourself is one of the greatest experiences you'll ever engage in simply because so often you're taught to modify who and how you are without really understanding why you are the way you are. Within you there's a vast world waiting to be explored and the only limit to how much you learn is up to you. There's always something more to discover and you should take every day as a challenge to discover how deep your waters go.

The mind and the body are there to be explored. Experience both and always push yourself to try new things in the pursuit of experience. Try a new restaurant. Try a dish that you've never tried before. Go to a supermarket and buy something from a country you don't even know where it is on a globe. If you have friends from different nationalities, ask them what typical dishes and drinks they enjoy.

Get to know how you perceive your surroundings. Focus on how your sense of touch varies from your forearm to your hand and your feet. Go to fabric stores and touch different textures. In short, basically engage full on with your senses and try to decipher how to describe what you feel, taste, hear, smell, or see. Your senses are an amazing gift and the human body is an incredible thing to experience.

When it comes to art, explore, branch out, see the influences of artists you love. Dig deep. Check for songs from soundtracks. Read what your favorite authors read. Read stuff you'd enjoy but also go to libraries and pick something you'd never have thought of checking out. Challenge yourself in as many ways as possible and when you're done with that set of challenges, realize that you can do this every day of your life. Life is to be lived and experienced, not merely survived. So do yourself a favor, and live.

Chapter 7:
Find your faith

Faith is not limited to religions.

People often think that faith is limited to those people who practice any sort of religion, when in reality, faith is the belief in something. Some people say they're atheist, but they believe in science or believe in their own power to do good.

But this chapter isn't about that. It's about finding your own faith, even if you practice a religion. There's something that's always resulted peculiar to me in regards to religions. A lot of people follow blindly, repeat blindly, and don't really internalize what they were brought up with. They also might identify themselves under a set of mores, but their behavior is actually at odds with what they supposedly believe. It's the equivalent to the phrase "preaching in your underwear." This goes from people who are part of a congregation as much as it falls to leaders in religious communities who talk a great game, but don't necessarily walk the walk.

The main thing is that part of religious doctrine is to scorn and punish any questioning. That's how things are because that's what one religious text says is so. Although I respect the right of every person to believe what they will, I do think it's worrisome that people don't question more often. Why are things such a way? What are the lessons in the stories we are taught? What is the value we are being taught in prayers we memorize? What is the message being offered and what does that message mean to me?

Such existential questions bother some people. I'm not

saying I don't understand why they bother; I'm saying that the fact that they bother people isn't unknown to me. That's because we strive for order for the familiar and for the routine because it's easier to repeat than it is to challenge.

As a child, I was brought up Catholic, studied at a Catholic school, did the First Communion, and regularly attended mass. I would scold my dad when he would say ungodly things while driving and I would confess that I killed a bunch of ants, accepting that saying 4 Our Holy Fathers would absolve me of sin.

When I was a teen, it was a very different story. For one part, I had several years where a lot of relatives passed away. I also almost drowned surfing and didn't see a white light and was faced with my mortality in several ways. I also experienced plenty of new types of heartbreak that were unknown to me. And of course, hormones.

Teen years are a rough ride because life kind of kicks into gear even though you still have no idea what real responsibilities are. As a teen, I would run my mouth and say that I was an atheist and that I had stopped believing in God. In hindsight, of course that was part of my rebellion in those formative years. But even as I said it, I didn't feel comfortable with it and it didn't feel that genuinely. I always said it angrily until I realized I was an atheist as a reaction. I had been Catholic because of my upbringing, but now that I knew better, phew! I wouldn't be so silly to... you can imagine the string of angst that would come from my mouth. Luckily, it didn't take long for me to learn better.

That's because when you see things that you don't understand, suddenly questions come upon you. Deep questions. Questions that would trouble you for years. And then one day, I found the definition of agnosticism: *an intellectual doctrine or attitude affirming the uncertainty of all claims to ultimate knowledge.*

As soon as I read it, something clicked. It's a good definition but in short, it's a fancy way of saying, I don't know, I'm not sure, and I wouldn't mind being OK with not knowing the answer to everything or being right when it came to my existence. That's how I see and experience agnosticism. Of course, I still have Catholic leanings because that's how I grew up and there are some great things to take away from a religion. But now I was comfortable having a conversation with God, no matter what it really ended up being. It could be me having a heart to heart with myself, or who knows? Maybe the message does arrive somewhere. What I do know is that words have power and so do conversations. By talking things out, I've been able to decipher plenty of things and that's one of the reasons why I talk so much and love to write. It's a way of deciphering and discovering myself.

It's not an easy way to live because I constantly have to explain my point of view and justify it on both sides of the debate, but I like living this way. I read texts (religious or otherwise) and allow them to mingle with my thoughts and opinions, and more often than not, good things happen.

As a kid, I read a lot of Chinese kung-fu comics. It's

another big part of who I am and to be honest, I adore them. But that also means I was exposed to aspects of Buddhism, Taoism, and Confucianism through what I was reading. It should come as no surprise that I often envisioned heaven being a board of deities trying to decipher what in the world we were doing to the world.

As an adult, the more I read, the more I find that a lot of religions have coexisting opinions, doctrines, and even characters and stories. It's a fascinating thing and is what has led me to believe that religions are different languages to translate and communicate the same core message. In addition, more often than not, religions are harmless in and of themselves. What's dangerous is how humans apply texts, teachings, and words. Words that might I add have been edited countless times, that have dozens and hundreds of versions, and that whose original meaning or at least some of the lessons might have been lost during the translation and editing process. When you see how people use religion to manipulate others and justify heinous actions, that's a sad sight. But on the flipside, when you see faith in action to heal people, to bring communities together, to mend wounds, and to inspire people to push beyond what they think they're capable of giving, well then you see the power of faith.

That said, faith has nothing to do with religion and everything to do with belief. Although religions can be defined as a set of beliefs, in reality, it's definition is more complex:

A set of beliefs concerning the cause, nature, and purpose of the universe, especially when considered as the creation of a superhuman agency or agencies, usually involving devotional and ritual observances, and often containing a moral code governing the conduct of human affairs.

So in essence, religions are nothing more than an agreed upon set of beliefs trying to explain what the hell is going on. There can be a god or gods. Angels are optional. Miracles are confirmed although not proven without a doubt. But still, it's nothing more than trying to figure out what happened, what's happening, and what will happen. And guess what? It remains anybody's guess.

People resort to science because it's provable and is based on facts. Indeed, science has helped us develop intellectually in increasing ways, although let us not be generous with all of ourselves. We preach the power and reach of science, yet have no idea how most technology works. Sure, we can learn about the process, watch a YouTube video on it or whatnot, but really understanding how things work eludes most people.

In addition, a lot of people put a lot of stock or all the chips on science, and although I do see the value and power of science, I can't help but remind that the basis of science is language and symbols, and if there's anything incomplete in this life, it's those two things. But apart from that, it also comes to my attention that science is a man-made method of explaining reality. It's measurable, quantifiable, theorized, and fascinating. But it's still a human explanation and last I checked, we're far from perfect.

So what is this chapter about anyways and how does creative kindness figure into this. Easy, the pursuit of knowledge should be a daily activity, but it should be done so humbly, accepting that what we accept as truth today could be tomorrow's punchline. How so? Well, think back to the belief that the world is flat and how odd it seems today (regardless of people who insist it still is). Now realize that once upon a time, that WAS the absolute truth and could not and should not be questioned. This was established by faith communities as well as by scientific or knowledge communities and it was nothing more than protecting their egos. Imagine preaching something your whole life only to be told that you were wrong? That's a powerful motivator to deter anything and anyone from going against what is true.

Paradigms exist but as technology evolves, the more paradigms succumb to new theories that are proved correct. So basically, we can understand until a certain level, until we break through to something else. So what if some of what we've learned in religion is true and fits into science? Why would that be a bad thing? Why would it be impossible? Why can't there be a dose of both in our approach to coping with life?

If life has taught me anything, it's that there's no weaker word than impossible, because all it takes is one exception to break that wall. So I choose to question as I search. I choose to accept the possibility of most things, because who knows what's possible? I know I don't, because I'm only human. But that isn't a bad thing. That's a choice. That's who I am. I'm not saying you have to be that way. I would never say that. But I will say that the more in control you are about what you believe and what you question, the easier it is to cope with how you choose to live.

This book talks a lot about choice and the power of choice. This chapter is no exception. Which is why I won't include a return of investment or summary section. Because that's up to you to write, if you choose to do so.

Chapter 8:
Cultivate your fields
of knowledge

Why aren't we learning more?

This sounds like a simple question, but in reality the intention is to shine a light on all the reasons why we're not as smart as we could be. Quite often, we humans are creatures of comfort and customs. Routine is rewarding because we don't have to push ourselves out of our comfort zones. The danger here is quite varied so why don't we begin by talking about the loss of trades and practical jobs.

Trades are being lost to technology and although some people can and do praise technological advances (as well we should), that doesn't mean we're getting any smarter. To put it more simply, while we learn more technological skills and are actually more adaptable to technology shifts, we're not necessarily smarter or better equipped to survive.

Many of us are baffled by how to fix faulty plumbing but we can download a new app and become an expert within days (if that). This example can be examined in thousands of ways. If we have to get to a location, we have no idea how to use a map, but we've long mastered how to follow directions from a GPS and how to shift from one location to another with a couple of taps or even voice commands. We have no idea how to light a fire but we can cook up a 15-minute meal with whatever is in the fridge thanks to a quick read and Pinterest.

When you see today's jobs, so many of them require an intricate knowledge of a complex set of functions within a system, but few of them require you to understand how that system even works. In addition, it's not like we're doing any sort of effort to make these jobs more appealing to younger generations. The saddest part is that there has never been a point in time where information and knowledge were more accessible. What's sadder still is that we've never lived in a time where it was easier to be distracted.

If you check current statistics, over 2 billion people worldwide own a smartphone of some sort. That basically means that over 25% of the world population has access to some version of the Internet. Depending on where you live, access is either wide open (think the US or Europe) or more restricted (refer to China or Korea to offer two examples). What doesn't change is that at arm's length you have access to information. LOTS of information. Yet somehow, 1/10 searches on the Internet are for pornography.

Please don't take this as an attack on pornography but rather an observation as to how we use the means we have available. Right now I'm writing on a computer with a smartphone next to me and a while back I was reading on an electronic reader. Earlier today I was watching a documentary while using an online TV subscription service. That's 4 ways in which I was exposed to information and the world at large. Was I always feeding my mind? Umm... no. I played games on apps and watched some videos that neither added nor took away from my life. In short, although I did learn a bit, I got entertained a lot.

Distraction is something common to pretty much all of us. Sure, we want to read a couple of things to sound fancy or even learn, but a lot of what we consume isn't necessarily to grow as a human, but to entertain us. It's not saying that we don't want to learn from fiction; heaven forbid such a thought. I've learned more from the Hobbit, the Sandman, Harry Potter, Dune, 1984, and comics than I have from some books that I was force fed as a child/teen/adult. But that doesn't change the fact that I'm easily distracted or that I don't know a lot of things. How does a lamp, a faucet, a CD, or a car work? I have no clue. But I do know how to use all of them rather well.

Which brings me to an important question, why don't *I* learn more? Why don't *you* learn more? Why are we so occupied with other things so often that the pursuit of knowledge is often ignored in favor of reaching a new level in a game or watching yet another cat video? Are we driven by distraction? Or is it something more; that we're also so exposed to so many things that the burden of decision inspires us to choose distraction over knowledge?

It's not to say there's no merit in reading a good book. Hell, I'm a writer so trust me I want at least a couple of people to enjoy reading a book if only for me to be able to do this type of thing more often. But what I do wonder is why don't I learn more every single day?

What's worrying is that I do like to learn random things and discover new things. I'm not saying I'm the most adventurous or inquisitive human this side of logic, but I'm definitely not average or subpar where curiosity is concerned. It's even more curious when I get a sense of enjoyment from what I learn and truth be told, I think I'd do pretty good in the JFK test. If you don't know what this means, think of this scenario: you're at JFK airport in New York and there's a flight delay of 4 hours. The test part comes in being interesting or tolerable enough to not have the person stuck with you at the airport on the verge of homicide or suicide. To be more succinct, it means having interesting stuff to talk about.

Upon writing that last line, maybe that yields some answers. Although its nature is debatable and it's more commonly attributed to Sir Francis Bacon, most people know the phrase "knowledge is power." By the same token, most people know the phrase, "with great power comes great responsibility," whose origins are often attributed to Uncle Ben, a father figure of a character who exists within the Marvel Universe, specifically the one pertaining to Peter Parker, better known as Spider-Man. Bacon was an English philosopher from the 16th and 17th century while Spider-Man is a comic book creation courtesy of Stan Lee and Steve Ditko from the 20th century.

This small explanation in the previous paragraph serves to explain two points:

1. **It is possible that we choose to be distracted to not have the responsibility to share knowledge**. Think about it, knowing things can actually be fun. Go to trivia night at a local restaurant if you want to see how many people agree with this statement. If you still need more proof, realize how many gameshows depend on the

knowledge a person possesses. Actually, some of these shows are based on exposing the lack of knowledge in an adult versus the intellectual prowess of a fifth grader. But what should we or can we do with that knowledge? Let it rot away? It's a shame to put such a good thing as knowledge in a drawer and not use it. Still, knowing things should instill in you a sense to tell someone about that information. Trust me, there have been plenty of locations where I've shared random knowledge and have been met with confused looks, because what did that have to do with anything related to the topic at hand (it happens more often than you think, trust me). But I've also been able to have 4-hour conversations with people who get my randomness and we can actually learn from each other while the dreaded head of boredom is nowhere to be seen.

Which brings us to the second point:

2. **There are lessons everywhere.** It's no accident that I followed up quoting an English scholar with a quote from a comic book.

Unfortunately, there is still a fear of learning... and I think it goes to a couple of more things. Firstly, we are taught by experience that learning is not only **not** fun, but that it is boring, a waste of time, and on occasion, even painful. Beyond that, we are taught that knowledge isn't necessarily something that makes us more attractive. It's not that intelligence is not sexy, it's that ripped abs, ample bosom, green eyes, luscious hair, and smoky eyes are something more obvious to appreciate. Sure, a valedictorian may make an impassioned speech that can inspire peers to push for excellence, but the football hero will be immortalized in a glass case forever more.

Many of these observations stem from external stimuli, i.e. how are you perceived and appreciated or rejected by your social circles. But there's also the inner aspect of knowledge. Unfortunately, knowledge also comes with a price, meaning that the more you know, the more you can possibly be affected by what's happening in the world. If you're ignorant to the rising levels of acidity in the oceans or the massive amounts of waste polluting both land and water, then recycling is an option you might not indulge in at every opportunity. If you don't know what child labor looks like, you'll always choose the bargain priced clothing without a second thought. If you know where your money is going, you won't stop donating to a well-known cause and won't need to research organizations that put your money to good use. These are just three arbitrary examples that serve to try and explain why we don't want to learn more and why we so often choose to get distracted.

If you browse social media platforms, the amount of bad news or just abhorrent behavior is common if not prevalent. Knowing the consequences of our actions or what's going on in the world and our communities, of course we choose to be distracted. There is power in escapism but there is danger too.

Whatever field you work in, there's a lot to learn about it. But there's a lot to learn about all sorts of wonders. From the history of things to how they actually work, there's no shortage of things that you can learn. The challenge is falling in love with learning and forgetting whatever muscle memory your brain has in regards to those crappy courses from grade school, high school, or college. The main thing is to find things that are interesting to you. Once you do that, branch out, learn more, and find ways to enjoy it. Afterwards, feel free to rinse and repeat. Most importantly, don't do it to impress anyone. Do it for yourself. Learn and love learning because it'll clear your vision in regards to passions you suspected or some you might have never even found if you didn't give that bit of randomness a go.

Furthermore, if you find something new to enjoy, who's to say you won't find more things to learn and enjoy. Who knows? You might even find that burning passion that can drive you for the rest of your life. But to do that, you have to step out of your comfort zone or you might even need to revisit old knowledge to look at it with new eyes.

That we look to be distracted is a reality and doing so from time to time isn't a bad thing. But we can't expect to grow as a species if we leave all the learning to other people or so-called experts. The reality is that those experts (worthy of the title or not) are happy the less you know, because that means more business for them.

The fact remains, there's a lot to learn and there are a lot of ways you can learn. Beyond that, learning is a wonderful thing. It enriches life and allows you to experience more and learn more. Besides, regardless of age, there's ALWAYS something to learn and by something, I mean millions of things. The best part is that every time you learn something about the world, you learn something about yourself, and we've already talked about how rich your inner topography already is. Imagine if you added more lands to explore?

Return of Investment

Learning is always a good thing, regardless of what we learned as kids, teens, and young adults. That we need a slight reminder of the wonders of learning isn't a bad thing, so by all means don't go beating yourself up because you have or haven't done something in the last couple of years. The only day we truly have full control of is today, although we can also plan for tomorrow. So let's focus on that and see what four reasons you can have to learn more every single day.

1.   KNOWLEDGE CAN MAKE YOU RICH

There are several ways this is true. In a corporate setting, the more you know the more you can be an asset to your company. This could come down to the way things are done, results you've seen, and experience that can save a company thousands or even millions of dollars. In specific terms, knowing the intricacies of something can make you such an expert that you can make an entire living off this.

I'm not a fan of over specialization, but that doesn't mean you can't be highly successful if you focus on all aspects of a single thing. Knowing how things work can help you capitalize on several situations and make a lot of money by being able to see the signs and make a savvy business decision. Again, I'm not big on this approach but I've seen it in practice on behalf of several people who make money off stocks and start-ups. They've learned to identify signs of opportunity and pounce and they enjoy it. This book isn't about judging so if that's your cup of tea, by all means, have it with some honey and cheers. Lastly, knowledge can make you rich because if something makes reality fascinating, it's worth investing in. I love knowledge and learning new things because it means I don't get bored, which is all too common in many people. Does that mean that learning things can make you happy? Well, I guess it does, but why don't you find out for yourself by giving it a try.

2. KNOWLEDGE HELPS YOU CONNECT WITH PEOPLE

Every single day is an invitation to grow in knowledge and worth, which actually helps you grow in empathy and understanding. It's not the same to try to relate to someone with a problem you have no information on than it is to know what people are talking about and options that they have in life. Part of that equation is definitely down to listening, but imagine understanding all that you're listening. That's the difference between having information and doing your best to help blindly. It is often said that knowing is half the battle but if you can win half the battle from the start, then that's a great asset to have on your side of any equation.

3. THE MORE YOU KNOW, THE MORE YOU GROW

Whether it's in your career or in who you are as an individual, knowledge, as it's defined, will add to who you are. You are not the same person you were before you learned X or Y thing, because knowledge impacts the way you view the world. Also, the more you know, the more open you are to learn more and judge less. And if you go back to chapter 4, you see that the less you judge, the happier you'll be. Imagine if you can judge less and learn more. Quite the combination you could put in play in regards to who and how you are.

4. IT BECOMES EVEN HARDER TO GET BORED

I can't help but marvel at the ease with which and the amount of people who get bored in their lives. Every single day there's something you can do and learn to ensure that boredom is never an option. People still don't see boredom as a choice, but it is and is often the laziest choice. So what'll it be? Have fun learning something new or stay in the comfort of old complaints?

SUMMARY AND TIPS:

How much you learn is always up to you and in life we get

to a point where it is completely up to us to either learn more or be content with what we have and stay nice and comfy and static. If instead you want to engage life and enjoy it, there's no shortage of things you can do for fun.

Start by re-reading stuff you learned in 3rd, 4th, and 5th grade and realize how little of it stuck. If you like to cook, explore different ingredients and techniques or find tips on how to perfect your favorite recipe. Are you tired of paying someone to fix plumbing, electrical fixtures, or holes in your clothes? Then learn something new.

Finding that something you're trying to learn is too hard? Then look for alternatives. Quitting is easy and shall always be an option, but there are always ways to help yourself learn better, be it with the help of people or on your own.

Another great aspect to consider is that learning new things often exposes you to new and interesting people who share your interests. Odds are that if you have an interest, there's a community who shares your passion or curiosity. What is the same is the desire to learn, which can be joyously infectious.

There are so many resources out there that you can also learn at your own pace, which is a refreshing alternative from the courses you took earlier in your life. Gone are the days where you have to cram and here are the days where you can take a leisurely pace or go full tilt. The choice is yours and we've already talked about how far choice can go in your life to bringing you joy.

Chapter 9:
Thoughts & actions

Helping people is something you can actually do, not something you simply wish for.

If that initial line sounds as if it has some extra bite, it's because it does. In a time where we are so connected and have so many options in regards to how we can help others, it's amazing how often we say something simply to ease our desire to help. Thoughts and prayers have gone from being something genuine to being the hackneyed response to the worst tragedies. If it sounds harsh to call it a cliché response, then it's even harsher to see it used ad naseum as if we don't have other options to do something to help.

Someone falls ill, someone loses a loved one, some tragic thing happens, and the best you can do is write *thoughts and prayers* in one social media post? That seems a bit odd to me especially with all we can do instead.

Please don't take this chapter as a bash on any religion or person. Instead, take it as constructive criticism to what ends up feeling like thinly veiled apathy. If all it takes to soothe your desire to help others it to write 18 letters in three words, then here's to low standards. Within your immediate reach, there are countless people who need help. In places you've visited at some point in your life, there are situations that could benefit from your intervention. Countries you've heard about are hurting at this very moment. People who you didn't know they existed could use any aid you send their way.

Is this to say you must support any and all causes? Certainly not. Doing so would not only leave you bankrupt, but miserable, and surely needing psychiatric help. Just in 2017, there were natural disasters courtesy of several Category 4 and 5 storms in the Pacific as well as the Atlantic Oceans. There have been earthquakes in Mexico, floods in Nepal and India, fires in California, Spain, Oregon, and Canada. There have been countless shootings, civil unrest, and countries are on the verge of war. It's a lot to take in, but remaining all cozy while tweeting thoughts and prayers and not engaging in some type of action speaks volumes to the times we live in.

The power of positive thinking and prayer is undeniable. It can and does make an impact, because it can inspire people to move. But if you *don't* move, if your good intentions remain in the realm of thought and theory, then I'm afraid to inform you that thoughts and prayers are in fact completely and utterly useless. Rather than the end results of efforts, thoughts and prayers should be taken as the pilot light which allows the flame to grow. Without the pilot light, there is no fire, but without fire and fuel, there is only a flicker and I do believe it's time we recognize the value of both.

THIS is why it's so important to bring forth *Thoughts & Action*. Because it begins in the realm of theory but reaches reality. It begins with wishful thinking but strives for results and not only results of the pieces landing where they may, but results that are impacted by our actions every single day. If you don't get involved, how do you expect there to be any change?

Do you know how many people are saved, fed, and clothed by thoughts and prayers? Not many to not say none. You know how many people are saved, fed, clothed, and healed through Thoughts and Action? Billions. Not dozens, hundreds, thousands, or even millions. **Billions.**

Unfortunately, settling has become as common as getting on our social media soapbox to bellow opinions but not do one thing to shift the needle in favor of what we so fervently believe in. It's troublesome to see how many people think clicking like on a post and writing thoughts and prayers and nothing else makes any sort of difference. If you're not sure if it does, let me be the one to tell you then, it doesn't. And we need to be told that in the face to see if we are jostled into action.

How often do we see someone who seems like they're down on their luck and could use a meal? How often does such a sight bring forth ideas to help them, buy them a meal or even spot them a cup of coffee? The answer is probably often but between that idea of helping and actually helping there's an important step we often don't take. It just takes putting ourselves out there, being human, engaging, caring... but that's a scary proposition.

What if the person is crazy? What if they're not down on their luck? What if it offends someone? What if they attack me? What if they use the money I give them for drugs?

The amount of rationalization that goes into NOT helping is an absolutely amazing thing to behold. I've done it and often have to fight against it. Sometimes I think it's the right call, sometimes otherwise and try to keep that in mind for the next opportunity to help someone. But if we don't ask, if we don't try, if we don't reach beyond our thoughts, that energy of good is not allowed the opportunity to bring forth positive change.

I will admit that I have a big problem with so-called mega churches and this is mainly to do because the pastors of said churches have a net worth of millions of dollars. Before reacting, see what I've just said, a pastor, a servant of Christ, someone who is supposed to be completely devoted to other people, has a *net worth*. They live in opulence. They own helicopters. They reside in mansions or estates. If you don't find anything at all at least peculiar about this, then maybe we read different versions of the Bible. In the one I read during my formative years, I didn't get the letter to the apostle St. Greed. I missed out on the fable of golden rings and exclusive palaces. I also didn't see the chapter where we worship a building more than we do our fellow human. But then again, maybe I'm reading the wrong bible (if such a thing is possible).

As you can see, I have a big problem with people who send out thoughts and prayers, pass out collection baskets, but are not only selective with the help they provide, but stingy.

Don't hold back the help you can give. If you can help someone and have the desire to do so, then do so. Embrace that pilot light and turn the gas up. Bring forth human warmth to the hearth of places who need that light and your help.

And also, and I can't stress this enough, don't do it to please or appease god. Do it because it's the right thing. Do it because it's within you to do so and you want to do so with nothing in return. Too often people play the quid pro quo game with actions. Some people do a lot of good but they do it to win a place in heaven. Although I'm thankful for their help and won't say "no thanks," part of me believes their action could have so much more of an impact if it came from a place where they didn't need a receipt for a good action. But again, if that's their way, at least they're helping. At least the impact they're doing is tangible. Is it genuine? Maybe not. But it's still a hell of a lot more than your typical thoughts and prayers.

Now imagine if you couple thoughts, prayer, and action. Imagine the change you can bring forth. I believe in the power of faith and in the power of people with strong faith. But I also believe in the power of people who don't believe in a god and who still want to do good because it's the right thing to do. Because they have an inherent need to not stand idly by. Because they want to help even if god isn't watching.

I often mention that I don't discriminate based on gender, race, religion, age, or any other classification, and that shall always be the case. I won't appreciate a devout person more than an atheist or vice versa. I shall appreciate the human beyond our particularities because we are all human. Regardless of where we live, how much we earn, the color of our skin, the nationality on our passport, the languages we speak, or the way we express our sexuality, we are human, and the best humanity has to offer should not and cannot remain in the realm of thoughts and prayers if we are to move along and survive, let alone thrive.

In short, measure your impact in life not by what you say but by what you do. Anyone in the world can send thoughts and prayers, but it takes a lot more to turn thoughts to action.

RETURN OF INVESTMENT:

This chapter is meant to break with previous chapters in terms of tone and content. It is not meant to offend but if one person is embedded with a dire need to help others, it is worth writing. That said, there are so many reasons why it's such a good idea to invest in Thoughts & Action and here are four of them:

1. YOU WILL DO INSTEAD OF WONDER

Too often we wonder if we could have done more to help. What would have happened if we'd just taken that step and done something? Could I have made a difference? These are horrible questions to carry... but if you allow action to flow from the pilot light of thoughts and prayers, you can do so much good that you'll amaze yourself.

2. YOU WILL GENUINELY FEEL GOOD ABOUT YOURSELF

Helping others has been clinically proven to be good for your emotional health. Don't take my word for it, look it up.

3. HELP HAS A WAY OF COMING BACK TO YOU

Consider it karma or the fact that someone might say they owe you a favor, it's amazing how often help comes back to you in unexpected ways.

4. YOU LEARN BY HELPING

It's amazing how much you can learn from helping others. When you participate in a donation drive or any community effort, there are literally dozens of things you can learn in a single day and there's always something new to learn and we've established how important and how good it is to learn, so soak it all up.

SUMMARY AND TIPS

It's easy to fall in a sense of complacency and apathy by not carrying forth the things that are within you. There is absolutely nothing wrong with thoughts and prayers, but we can't let that be our end game. It has to be the warm up because leaving things in the realm of thoughts is a waste of positive energy that can mold the world.

If you feel you've sent too many thoughts and prayers, reach out to the people, offer a friendly ear or maybe even a shoulder to cry on. There is a LOT you can do and here's where creative kindness figures in. Look at a situation that inspires you to want to help and analyze and determine how many ways you can help. Order your options in terms of the impact you can have, contact the right people, and go for it. Keep an eye out for opportunities to help and engage with whatever you do so that good intentions get through as powerfully as possible.

Some people think sharing a post or important and verified valuable information isn't much, but it can actually save a life. The most important thing is to verify before sharing. In these times, this is key and will also go a long way into ensuring that you not only offer valuable information, but that when you do share something, people will listen or read. Don't limit yourself to wishing and thinking, do. The inception of change is thought, but the results come from action.

Chapter 10:
Listen instead of just waiting for your turn

A lot of people in the world don't really listen and you don't have to be one of the bunch.

Listening is an art in and of itself. It's also something a lot of people don't do or their approach to it is a bit odd, to say the least. When it comes to communication there are several issues that come between you and the best conversation possible. The first one is actually yourself while a second one can definitely be the distractions we face in any given situation on any given day. Let's take a look at each.

YOU IN CONVERSATION VS. YOU AND SOMEONE ELSE

Too often people are just waiting for their turn to talk in a conversation. It's an odd thing but it's actually quite common. By this, please understand that the person is actually only marginally paying attention and maybe taking the barest of notes to be engaged in the conversation. It's something you tend to notice after repeated times where people say or ask something you were actually just talking about.

So first off, stop only focusing on what you have to say. A meaningful conversation may include a person baring parts of who they are either to share a story, look for support, or even ask for advice. The least you can do is pay full attention.

By the way, this is presuming that we're having an amicable conversation so maybe the example is clearer when there is some type of conflict, but we'll take a look at that a bit further on within this chapter. In this example, it's all about focusing on what you have to say or what you want to say instead of what the person in front of you is saying.

In my experience, the more attention you pay to what someone has to say, the more you can help and the more it shows. Trust me, people really appreciate when you pay attention to the details, those shared, and those hinted at. Sometimes people limit to reacting to what someone has to say and only focus on spoken language when right in front of them people are saying something that either adds or even possibly contradicts what they're saying. Unfortunately, if you mainly focus on what you will say when it's your turn, you'll easily miss these details. And if that's not bad enough, imagine when you add the fact that we're bombarded by distractions.

THE OUTSIDE WORLD BARGING IN
There are SO many distractions all around that it's easy to allow them to come between you and a conversation. At one point or another, we get distracted and saying you never get distracted is at the very least pretty tough to believe and insanely hard to accomplish, but we have to accept the possibility of that happening.

Maybe you're tired, maybe there's a ton of noise all around, maybe someone keeps texting you or the person who you're talking to, maybe you remember that thing you left at your friend's house the other day. The amount of mental chatter we endure on the daily is insane and if you add real world chatter, no wonder it's so hard to pay attention sometimes.

It's very possible that it all comes down to caring and keeping yourself in check. If you're in a home or any sort of quiet place, that's where you have the most control over your surroundings, which means you can put the phone in another room, turn off TVs, and eliminate as many sources of distraction as possible. In public, it's harder, because it's not like you can turn off all the TVs in a pub or tell everyone in a restaurant to shut up. What you CAN do is choose where you have that conversation and "Let's get out of here so we can chat properly" is a powerful statement that's always up for use if wherever you are talking at isn't working for you. It also sends a clear message to the other person: "you matter and I want to give you my full attention."

If the phone is doing its thing, turn it the hell off. Seriously. The great distractor of our times is the phone. We all know it's wonderful but it's also as disruptive as it is addictive. Some restaurants actually have no phone policies trying to get people to enjoy each other's company for a change. You know, like the good ole times where you didn't care about WiFi reception and focused on whether the food was good or not. Sure they want you to consume more, but the fact that we're always paying attention to what's next on the to-do list speaks a lot about how we treat the present. The main issue many of us are facing is that the present is the only time we're alive and if we're distracted from it, of course we won't engage properly and miss out on life.

The issue at hand is that even so, we can still get distracted when engaging in a conversation. One possibility is that we do this as a defense mechanism. We endure so much bad news on any given day that we often tend to hungrily seek out distractions in the hope of smoothening or drowning out the bad news we've already endured. That said, even when we're engaged we seek distraction or we worry we're missing out on something, which can be a good thing.

MISSING OUT ON SOMETHING ISN'T BAD

A lot of what we do is out of fear that we're missing out on something. That's why we check social media so much, which is odd. Our treatment of social media is the equivalent of channel surfing between several channels. Sure, we can have an idea of what's happening on each channel but we will lose valuable information from one or probably several of the things we're watching. You can even have five TVs in front of you, which isn't that uncommon in way too many places for it to be OK. If you don't believe me, check how many screens you have at the gym, at a restaurant, and elsewhere. Now imagine turning off all other stimuli and focusing on one TV. Don't you think you'd better understand what's happening and get the full message?

Actually, while writing this chapter I'm fighting hard to

not be distracted. I've closed all other web browsers, I've set the phone out of my reach, and even so, the mental chatter is having a party trying to distract me from this chapter. More than a medical condition, it's a sign of the times we're living. But sometimes we need to remind ourselves we are more in control than how we behave. That we're so easily distracted can happen... but that we act powerless in front of the situation, well that's just an odd way of going about things.

Are we really that weak versus distractions? Can we not focus on a single task for ten minutes? Must we live multitasking lives? That's the point though. We're so obsessed with being in every conversation that we forget to focus on the one we're in. What's interesting is that when we DO focus on single tasks, we become ultra-engaged and obtain amazing results, which should make us wonder why we can't be that way every day with every single activity we engage in or at least a bit more often. There's nothing stopping us except irrational fears and addictions. So how do we tackle those?

Firstly, if you miss out on something, what will happen? Will someone die? Will you lose money? Will your performance be impacted negatively? Quite simply, no. You'll not know something and want to know something. This is actually a great thing. You know why? Because it means you have something to talk about with other people. Sometimes we forget that not knowing things is downright wonderful. In previous chapters, we've established that learning every day is a great thing and it's true. It's fantastic. But you don't need to learn everything on your own. You don't have to have ALL the information.

Unfortunately, there's a fear that not being in the know will mean we're either stupid, or out of the loop, and we are terrified of being embarrassed so much that we opt for trying to tune into everything. This learned behavior spills over into other parts of your life, hence that hunger to know everything and do as many things as possible.

What has been hinted at this entire chapter is that we've lost sight of the power of focus and the value of it for that matter. It doesn't matter how many examples we see of how amazing focus can be, the reality is that a lot of us forget the rewards that can be reaped from this practice. If you see someone shooting an arrow, you know the importance of focus. It's the difference between hitting the target or losing in a competition, or worse yet, putting someone in danger.

Conversations greatly benefit from this treatment for several reasons. The only request is for you to not get creepy with the focus because if someone's trying to tell you something, getting stared at isn't going cut it and will actually scare a person off because it makes it hard for them to say what they have to say. That said, you can still help your focus in several ways. We've talked a bit about external stimuli, but what about while engaging in the conversation.

Something recommended for patients AND doctors during a visit is to repeat what is being said in the form of a question and go from there to make sure everyone is understanding what is being said (it's the difference between following directions and nodding for approval without understanding what is being said).

In a hypothetical conversation, let's suppose that during your chat someone says a car is red. You can say in return, "so you're telling me the car is red. What importance does that have?" If it sounds like something a shrink would do during psychotherapy sessions, odds are that you're not mistaken. It's a technique to make sure you understand the information being shared while still digging deeper into what is being shared. Conversation is often about digging, observing, sharing, and then digging some more. The interesting part is that sometimes asking a question like the one above can lead to a breakthrough. Think about it, that single question could easily lead to several answers.

1. The color doesn't matter! What matters is who was driving it.
2. It's such a lovely color. It reminds me of Tommy.
3. Oh! It's not important, it got my attention and for some reason I wanted to share it. What is important is that...

Any of these answers is a plausible path to a conversation. All can lead to bits of information that can help things flow along and allow you to be engaged with whomever you're talking with. Think about those conversations that wind along for hours because you lost track of time and then think about the ones where even 5 minutes feels like an eternity. Although chemistry has a lot to do with it, you don't have a say in that. What you do have a say in is in the approach you take with a conversation.

I think about some conversations I have and how they flow and I see patterns with certain people. How I avoid topics with some people, how I always look for certain topics with others, and how with some people I can just waffle for hours without a care in the world. In those last conversations, you realize that you don't pander, you don't limit yourself, you're completely honest, and you always find something else to talk about and quite effortlessly at that. If you look at that friendship and those conversations, you realize that you went from taking your basic approach to a conversation and eventually molded it into something that only you share with that person, and THERE is a huge secret to having more meaningful conversations.

DISCOVERING COMMON GROUND

For a conversation to elevate to a next level, to be something more than chatter, you have to find that special something you share with someone. To understand more clearly, imagine having three distinct conversations about the same topic with three different people. Notice how much the approach, the tone, and the rhythm of the conversation can change from one person to another. Realize that this is the result of you putting away the notion that you will have the same conversation with each person. Now read that last sentence again.

TOO often we try to have the same conversation with people and offer the same advice without taking the extra step of seeing how it applies to their situation. The reality is that every conversation is like a wave. It might break similarly, but it is always different because the context in which it occurs is different from the rest. Even seeing the most consistent surf breaks shows that there are variations in each wave. Maybe the wind hit it differently, maybe there was more water in the sandbar or reef, maybe the tide was a bit higher or lower. The amount of varying factors is astonishing and conversations are the same. Even something as simple as switching coffee for tea or beer during the conversation can have an impact and make it vary from one person to the next. That's a beautiful thing because otherwise you're reading a script and you're once again waiting for your turn to deliver lines, that no matter how well they're written and delivered, will lack the power of a true conversation, which is as much about what is being said as what is being shared.

For an even clearer example, think of those times you have to contact a call center. What's the difference between a good representative and one who isn't? Engagement. When I've spoken to a rep that shows that they care about my situation, that they're paying attention, and are even kind of emotionally invested, good things happen. If instead you get the person who hates their job, is bored, doesn't care, and lets it show, how do you think that conversation goes?

Now think about that scenario again. This is a person's job. They have to have lord knows how many conversations on a given day to meet their quota. What marks the biggest difference between a great sales rep and some average Josephine or Joe is that one only looks at the quota and the other prefers to focus on the person who needs to resolve a situation, rather than obsessing over metrics. Guess who's going to make a better impact. I'm not saying who's going to solve the situation or who meets the quota better. They might all be well and capable of resolving your situation, the less pleasant rep might be killing it at the numbers game, but which one will leave a lasting impression? Which one will you wish you get if you ever have to call again?

The same applies to conversations in life. The more engaged you are, the more you care, the less you focus on the clock and focus more on listening and caring, the more meaningful that connection will be. Also of note, this isn't a one-time thing, but if it were, what memory do you want to leave as a result of that conversation.

I'm blessed with an abnormal ability to waffle on and on, but even so, I like to do my best to treat every conversation as the most important thing at any given time. And yes, even when I'm having multiple conversations online. And here is another super important point to make.

ONLINE BEHAVIOR SHOULDN'T REPLACE REAL LIFE

I talk to quite a few people on any given day and do my best to engage with them genuinely. This could be in comments on social media, via text, phone calls, or in real life. I come from a time where chatrooms were a thing, but even so, I've known to carry upwards of 10 conversations simultaneously. Firstly, I don't recommend doing this because eventually the joke from one conversation can offend someone in another. It's something I stopped doing because I realized that although fun, it wasn't practical.

Even so, I can still have multiple conversations online simply because of the nature of it. I bring this point to the table because I'm sure I'm not the only one. I also know I'm not the only one who has been chatting with someone while watching YouTube videos, playing a game online, drinking tea, and filling out time sheets.

Multi-tasking is something that's beyond commonplace nowadays but we NEED to realize that online *behavior* should be left *online*. That whole getting distracted stuff we've been talking about is nothing more than us transferring behavior from one environment to another. Life on and offline are two very different things and although we can nurture wonderful friendships on both mediums, we have to accept that they're different. Otherwise, you run the risk of getting into a discussion because you're not paying full attention to one thing or another, which brings us to discussions.

WINNING ISN'T ALWAYS A WIN

For some reason or another, we are obsessed with winning. Our team is the best, our favorite band is the best, my writing style, musical style, vocal approach, or recipe is the best. And where there's a discussion, we NEED to win.

I've seen this in the flesh way too many times to ignore that winning an argument isn't necessarily the best outcome of a discussion. When people are focusing on winning, they take a sports approach, they look for weaknesses and attack. Although this tactic can win a fight, a game, or a business venture, quite often it does more damage than good to relationships of all types.

It's not an easy thing to turn off that instinct that says "attack," but the more I do it, the better I get along with people in all environments. The main thing about winning is that it's all about ego and ego is a dangerous thing to not keep in check. It's probably a given that we all know a person who needs to win *always*. What's curious is how often these people aren't really happy even if they win the most or even if they happen to win all of the time.

That's because winning at life takes a lot more than a check mark in the win column. Life is not black and white and as humans, we have endless layers to explore. But if we solely focus on winning, that cuts out our ability to even find common ground, let alone to nurture it. It isn't easy taking hit after hit while asking for an amicable environment to occur. Sometimes it's in your face, sometimes it's passive aggressive, but it always has consequences.

My experience has shown me that when you drop the ego and talk and express yourself honestly and take any and all criticism as part of the dialogue, great things can happen. I'm not perfect and the truth is that I have plenty of areas of opportunity, particularly with certain topics where opposing sides come out guns a blazing. But I'm learning and every day I learn to engage in meaningful dialogue to ensure my point is being understood as much as I am understanding the other side's view. The more I do this, the more I learn that to be a winner in life (as I understand it), you have to care less about winning and more about connecting and understanding. It's taken many wins and losses to learn this, but it's also allowed me to focus on common ground instead of conquered territories. That's because when winning isn't the goal, everyone wins.

RETURN OF INVESTMENT:

Listening is one of the most powerful albeit underused skills we have because of mentalities focused on winning rather than resolving. Distractions exist all around but we can rise above and beyond them to show that as humans we are in control. Here are four reasons why listening more can be one of the best decisions in your life.

1. YOU GET MORE INFORMATION

Getting all the information from a conversation is

impossible. There's always things either forgotten or omitted, but when we pay attention and don't merely wait for our turn to talk, we get the full message instead of settling for fragments. Information can contain the solutions we need or maybe it can inspire a question that will lead to the best result. By also listening more, you see that the conversation becomes about the people involved more than one party over another.

2. YOU AVOID BEING A KNOW IT ALL

Learning from others is a wonderful thing but some people love knowing it all. Unfortunately, being a know it all is rarely if ever seen in a positive light. Contrast these two images: someone who knows everything and constantly corrects people and someone who knows a lot but always finds something new to learn in what you say. Connecting comes about beautifully when we learn from each other and it teaches you to pay attention to what young kids and older people have to say, because knowledge doesn't discriminate and there's plenty to learn from everybody if we focus on listening.

3. YOU REPLACE WIN FOR WIN-WIN

Resolutions are powerful and last much longer than a win. It means a true resolution was sought rather than a victory. Weaknesses do not get exploited although they can be discussed, which can yield so much for all the parties involved. The age-old adage of it takes two to tango is as real as you let it be. Fighting takes two people willing to engage in an argument for it to occur. It's easy to take your gloves off and go for the kill, but if instead one person opts to engage in a conversation to find a resolution and the other person follows suit, every single time will have better results than a win.

4. WE ARE ENGAGED

Rather than have time fly by, we are able to engage with what we're living much more fully. Suddenly you see details about different things and start learning things you would have otherwise overlooked.

SUMMARY AND TIPS

At the beginning of this chapter, we mentioned that listening is an art in and of itself. This is completely true because how we listen today is not how we listened 3 years ago or how we will listen 10 years in the future. It's an ever-evolving tool and skill that can have good moments and bad. The last statement is more or less a way of letting you know that learning to listen doesn't mean we'll listen every single time.

Some people lose sight of the impact proper listening can have on their lives and reminding themselves of the importance of proper listening can go a long way in ensuring they don't get frustrated by repeating mistakes they thought they'd even forgotten how to commit. Will we still make age-old and even "classic" mistakes? Of course! I often say we're not perfect but beyond that, we're stubborn for the silliest of things. Knowing what we're capable of means we can keep ourselves in check and keep an eye out for knee-jerk reactions. I've caught myself many a time reacting as I would have 10 years ago. Sometimes I catch myself after I've let go of the reaction, but at least I'm aware and remedy as soon as I can.

As for tips, the main thing about paying attention is all about controlling where you are, what distractions there are, and how you can either ignore, minimize, or mitigate them. If a place is too distracting, say so. Try and find a place where talking can be done easily and where you and the other person are both comfortable. It can be anywhere, a restaurant and a coffee place may be common, but a simple walk around the block can do wonders for connecting with someone.

Also, while talking, ask questions about what is being said. This not only shows you're paying attention but will help you internalize what is being talked about and in the meantime will even help you get to know the other person, which is always a good thing. Lastly, care about what is being said more than about what you want to say about the situation. Too often we focus on our lines rather than what is being shared, and common ground shall always be about the latter.

Chapter 11:
Teamwork teaches
creative kindness

Although lots of people don't like teamwork, it's one of the best ways to learn and apply creative kindness.

Every fellow human needs help at one point or another. Even the most independent individual will need help during a health crisis or possibly to assist one person that needs not one but two people to survive. Case in point: a person trained in CPR can save a life, true. But guess what; two people trained in 2-person CPR attending the same person in need have an incredibly higher success rate. This isn't speculation, it's a fact you can easily verify. What's the catch? Both people need to know how to work the 2-person CPR technique to ensure the best results.

Now you might be saying that the above example is a bit drastic, but often times drastic examples show the point that is being made as clearly as possible. CPR is a basic technique we should all know to some degree and quite honestly refresh as often as possible. During a training I participated in a couple of years back, I saw this 2-person technique and could clearly see the benefits of it as well as the challenges it can bring. When it comes to this scenario, there is no nitpicking, the person closest to the head focuses on breathing while the person closest to the chest focuses on compressions. The idea is to ensure people don't fatigue and that they can keep CPR going at maximum effectivity for as long as possible.

The absurdly vast majority of situations in your life will not come down to saving the life of a person unless you work in related fields. Most of us won't even need to use

CPR, the Heimlich maneuver, or other life saving techniques. But there are several points to be made with the CPR example.

SOMEONE WAS PAYING ATTENTION

The fact that CPR saves lives is undeniable. That it does not have a 100% success rate is reality. So someone looked at the process of administering CPR and tried to figure out how to improve something that was already working. CPR is often a multi-tasking technique where you have to alternate between compressions and inhalations. (Some people might say that compression-only CPR is more effective, but that's nitpicking for this example and there are stats for and against this point). By separating the actions and assigning each to one person, focus can be given fully to each action rather than alternating. It is also less physically taxing to share responsibilities, which goes for most any scenario.

Although this may make some sense to many of you, it is quite possible that other group dynamics are knocking at your memories to remind you of how wonderfully ineffective, frustrating, and toxic team scenarios can be. For a common example, think of group projects in school and college. It's VERY rare for someone to have only fond memories of group projects. I for one have several "horror" stories and I'm sure a lot of people will find them familiar. That person who vanished off the face of the Earth. The slacker. The person who needed to call the shots and bully everyone to have things their way even if they weren't the best. And yes, the people who you got along with.

Group dynamics are a peculiar thing and I've been in enough teams and had enough jobs to know the clear difference between good work and wars of attrition. As a group member, I believe I'm wayyyyyyyyyy better now than 2, 5, 10, and 15 years ago. It takes a lot of mistakes to learn but by listening and seeing how I could be my best in most any scenario, I've gotten to the point where I can contribute to most groups to some degree or so I at least strive to be.

So the first thing you need is the desire to learn and to learn to work with others. We all have methods to our madness and that's not a bad thing, but silo mentalities and being inflexible are also common things people engage in. The first thing we need to do is recognize that there are a TON of ways to classify people, groups, and members of a group.

This is so complex that people make a living out of explaining personality traits, group dynamics, and how to improve or understand individuals within and removed from group contexts. It's all a lot of business talk but there is sense to what experts in this field share.

The easiest way to begin seeing how you can learn from a group is having an idea of who and how you are. For me particularly, I'm not a fan of labels be they based on zodiac signs, nationality, or personality types. I think it is actually limiting, but that's my perspective. Other people find it liberating to have a label that allows them to understand who and how they are a bit better.

I learned a bit about this by seeing people identify themselves as INFJ, ENFJ, or some other combination of cryptic letters that confused the hell out of me. Upon doing some digging, it seems that according to certain experts from Consulting Psychologists Press, Inc., there are 16 personality types. That's a nice chunky number and it offers enough variety for you to search to see which fits you best.

Here's a summary of the personality types and the definition of the acronyms with a brief explanation in parenthesis according to Bryers-Miggs:

ISTJ - Introverted Sensing Thinking Judging
(Introverted Sensing with Extraverted Thinking)

ISTP - Introverted Sensing Thinking Perceiving
(Introverted Thinking with Extraverted Sensing)

ISFJ - Introverted Sensing Feeling Judging
(Introverted Sensing with Extraverted Feeling)

ISFP - Introverted Sensing Feeling Perceiving
(Introverted Feeling with Extraverted Sensing)

INFJ - Introverted iNtuitive Feeling Judging

(Introverted Intuition with Extraverted Feeling)

INFP - Introverted iNtuitive Feeling Perceiving
(Introverted Feeling with Extraverted Intuition)

INTJ - Introverted iNtuitive Thinking Judging
(Introverted Intuition with Extraverted Thinking)

INTP - Introverted iNtuitive Thinking Perceiving
(Introverted Thinking with Extraverted Intuition)

ESTP - Extraverted Sensing Thinking Perceiving
(Extraverted Sensing with Introverted Thinking)

ESTJ - Extraverted Sensing Thinking Judging
(Extraverted Thinking with Introverted Sensing)

ESFP - Extraverted Sensing Feeling Perceiving
(Extraverted Sensing with Introverted Feeling)

ESFJ - Extraverted Sensing Feeling Judging
(Extraverted Feeling with Introverted Sensing)

ENFP - Extraverted iNtuitive Feeling Perceiving
(Extraverted Intuition with Introverted Feeling)

ENFJ - Extraverted iNtuitive Feeling Judging
(Extraverted Feeling with Introverted Intuition)

ENTP - Extraverted iNtuitive Thinking Perceiving
(Extraverted Intuition with Introverted Thinking)

ENTJ - Extraverted iNtuitive Thinking Judging
(Extraverted Thinking with Introverted Intuition)

That said, according to R. Meredith Belbin, there are nine types of team roles that we could also explore in a group setting, which are: **Shaper**, **Implementer**, **Completer**, **Coordinator**, **Team worker**, **Resource investigator**, **Evaluator**, **Specialist**, and **Innovators**.

If you dig further, you can even find the seven personality groups that make a well-rounded team, courtesy of Tatyana Sussex, which are: **Leader**, **Team player**, **Researcher**, **The Expert**, **The Planner**, **The Creative**, and **The Communicator**.

The Zodiac is divided into the following astrological signs: **Aries**, **Taurus**, **Gemini**, **Cancer**, **Leo**, **Virgo**, **Libra**, **Scorpio**, **Sagittarius**, **Capricorn**, **Aquarius,** and **Pisces**.

For us wizarding geeks, it's not uncommon to classify ourselves as **Gryffindor**, **Hufflepuff**, **Slytherin**, or **Ravenclaw** according to the Wizarding World of Harry Potter as created by JK Rowling.

As you can see, there's no shortage of ways to classify ourselves, but that doesn't change the fact that playing nice with others isn't as easy as we'd like it to be. So why all the labels mentioned above? Well, there are several reasons we can explore to show how complex group dynamics can be and how you can decipher the mysteries of getting along while doing the thing, and doing it kindly AND creatively.

1. KNOW THE LANGUAGE YOUR TEAM SPEAKS

I could go into detail about the categories explained above, but people have already done it and besides, that's their intellectual property, so it's best to go to the source rather than an indie author who quoted brilliant people to offer context to the point I'm trying to make. That said, it's good to read about the predominating traits with the labels so that you can understand where someone is coming from in regards to how they see themselves and the terminology they use to identify the way they are and how they work. It's not the same to deal with an INFJ than it is to deal with a Libra or a Hufflepuff. By also learning about their preferred language, you can connect better with people and the best way to get to work with people is by showing you care enough about them to learn about what matters to them.

2. DISCOVER YOURSELF BY LEARNING ABOUT OTHERS

It's amazing what we can learn about ourselves by hearing how others think about different things or by how they view themselves. Regardless of how unique we are, we share traits and sometimes we read or listen to something that is so "us" that we can't help but nod. It's always good to be sure of who you are, but by being flexible in regards to what identifies you as you, you can dig ever deeper and find the essence of who you are. That's because introspection may be an essential part of how we find ourselves, but by interacting with others and adding to who we are, it is quite possible we can lead even richer lives.

3. BE OPEN TO NEW IDEAS

An essential part of learning comes from being open to things you're not used to or more so allowing yourself to consider perspectives or opinions different from your own. It's not easy being open to new things. It's possibly a combination of fear of losing the essence of who we are coupled with resistance based on what we think without even knowing about a topic. It's almost like trying a new dish. A lot of people eat the same things over and over and don't try things because they don't think they will like them. The kicker is that if you don't try, you'll never know and in my life, I can tell you of hundreds of things I've tried and enjoyed immensely. I'm from Puerto Rico. I have no business eating sushi from a socio-cultural perspective. That said, I loved it from the first time I tried it and not only that, I always love trying new sushi. At this point in time, my favorite is sea urchin and if I had to describe its flavor I'd go for sweetish ocean water pudding. In short, it's weird, but it sends my taste buds soaring. Now, if I hadn't tried it, I wouldn't have discovered how much I love it. Well the same goes with knowledge, information, science, literature, movies, art, and music. Judging without engaging is a popular way of limiting ourselves and it serves no purpose. Also not listening to a side of the argument you don't agree with isn't productive either. I'm not saying it's easy, but most times it's completely worth it to listen to people. In the end, everything you learn can add to who you are.

4. ACCEPT PEOPLE HOW THEY ARE

The biggest challenge when dealing with a group is accepting people as they are. This doesn't mean you'll stand by if they're slacking, but working to someone's strengths rather than wanting to force them to change is among the options you have available. Wanting to mold people so that they work in the style you work is a waste of energy and time. Sure, a person may eventually change, but then you'll have to focus on what you have to do while also supervising what they're supposed to be doing and ensuring they're doing it to your standards. Acceptance, on the other hand, can allow you to work with the person to see how you can get them to be their best even if that's different from what you think would be the ideal.

CREATIVE KINDNESS IN A GROUP SETTING

When it comes to group settings, creative kindness comes in the way you understand and interact with others. How you can do the best work with one person is not the same as with another and is not the same as if you combine more people into the equation. It takes a lot of patience and objectivity to try and give your best in whatever role you land and to assist others to give their best. To do this you don't have to be the alpha or any specific role though. Some people can't talk if it isn't with their pride and that's something you might have to deal with, but the ego is their problem. Your problem is how to use that ego to the best advantage of the team and that answer will be different every single time you ask questions to address that situation. That's because being human, that means that what works today might not work tomorrow and something that has never worked might suddenly work. We're ever changing, ever shifting, ever evolving, and being aware of this reality will allow us to use whatever resources we have to ensure that kindness prevails and results are obtained.

RETURN OF INVESTMENT

Group settings aren't always easy but group dynamics can be immensely enriching. You just have to get in the right mindset for it and take each challenge as a lesson to learn from.

1. ACCEPTANCE BRINGS THE BEST FROM PEOPLE

One of the biggest things people don't realize is that when you accept someone the way they are you are giving them the opportunity to share their best with you. The less we judge and the more we work to the strengths of a person, the better the results everyone will be able to enjoy.

2. YOU LEARN FROM EVERY INTERACTION

Everyone is different and every interaction can yield new lessons because experience is a constant state of learning if you wish it to be. How something affects someone or how you can better understand different people will go miles upon miles to helping you understand yourself and have more options for future interactions.

3. YOU ARE NEVER A ONE TRICK PONY

Being good is one thing, knowing how to be good in more than one setting is another. Looking at situations from more than one angle yields options and when you have options, you can choose what best fits for any given situation. In short, the more you live, the more you can learn, and the better you can be and being your best and inspiring the best from different people. Some people specialize in one thing or perfecting one approach. That's commendable and can be very valuable. But what happens when your Ace doesn't work in a scenario. Having options is empowering but learning how to choose the best option and not get stuck in thinking is something else to learn and continually perfect.

4. EGO CAN STEP OUT OF THE WAY

Although some people are the "my way or the highway" type, which is sometimes necessary, not letting ego get in the way of you and learning a lesson has proven to be just as worthy as an approach to life. Some people need to run on ego to get things done, but when you focus on results and on inspiring people to focus on their strengths and improve areas of opportunity, you can build others as you build yourself.

SUMMARY AND TIPS

Creative kindness need not be limited to a single player scenario. Sure, a lot of people like to walk to the beat of their own drum, but playing in a band can be so much fun and so rewarding. The main thing is to always ask yourself if you're giving people all the opportunities to share the best they have to offer. If there's a but in the answer, then how can you impact the dynamic to ensure the person feels safe to share their best and go for it because you have their back.

If you find you're not understanding someone or you're butting heads, try and see what's coming in between you and the goal. Is it a clash of personality? Is it fear? Is it a problem in communication? The possibilities are endless but the more you try to find what's the issue, the better options you'll have.

People are often afraid to be their true selves or to be judged because of a mistake and that's a recipe for subpar results. If instead the person knows that you have their back, that a mistake won't be the end of the world, then trust me, they'll swing for the fences and not recklessly either. Acceptance can empower people and that's another reason why judging others can come between you and great things.

Some people would opt to live a completely isolated life and that's an option, for sure. But if you want to get along better with others, dispense with judging. Will that mean people won't judge you? Not at all, but that's their problem and a LOT of people have that problem. But just because other people do it, doesn't mean you should too.

Acceptance isn't easy but quite often it's immensely rewarding. If you're not sure about it, then give it a try. Who knows? You might surprise yourself and others.

Chapter 12:
Own your faults while rising above them

Although tendencies would say otherwise, accountability **never** goes out of style.

It's curious that so often people seek to pin the blame on other people. Sometimes it's because it is the fault of others, but sometimes, and quite often, it's more on the lines of people never wanting to be wrong or fearing the consequences of owning a mistake. Well, let me tell you something, owning to my mistakes has never put me in a situation I cannot respond to. I'm not saying it's pleasant or fun or a jolly good time. I'm saying it's never put me at a disadvantage. Actually, quite the contrary.

You see, when you admit fault and seek to rectify it, that means several things. For starters it means you take the situation seriously and want to help in any way shape or form to ensure that it is resolved promptly. Secondly, it takes character to own a mistake and correct it. Some people think it'll go on some sort of mythical record and that one day, judgment shall fall upon them fiercely and mercilessly. If that sounds a bit much, it's because it is.

We're human. Mistakes are part of what makes us human and a mistake can teach you plenty of things if you can get past the embarrassment. This is easier said than done since we are mostly terrified of embarrassment. As humans, life teaches most of us to avoid pain and seek pleasure or gratification. So imagine how bad embarrassment is for us to avoid even the risk of it.

That said, sometimes we need a kind reminder that mistakes aren't the end of it all. Getting embarrassed, privately or publicly, doesn't mean you're done for the rest of your life. You know why? Because as long as there is a breath in your body, there is another chance, another opportunity to rectify a mistake or rise above it.

Unfortunately, some people learn early on that blaming someone else is not only allowed, but good for them, because it avoids you looking anywhere near vulnerable, and vulnerability is something that many of us hide for one reason or another. Maybe we fear people will see weakness and seek to take advantage. Maybe it has to do with being taught that we have to be strong for others and that any sign of weakness will bring harm or worry to others. But blaming is one of the worst things you can learn to be good at. Not because you won't get results, or riches, or even success, but because deep down, you'll know it's all a farce or any success you have will come with an asterisk, which will probably inspire you to be even more defensive when it comes to the topic of accountability.

For me, accountability has not been a detriment. Instead, facing consequences for mistakes has empowered me in several ways. Firstly, I've lost the paralyzing fear of committing a mistake. I'm not saying I welcome mistakes with open arms, but if they happen, I know I'm not powerless against them. Instead, I learn from them and some of the mistakes that have stung the most are some of the lessons I've learned the most from. Does that mean that mistakes are a good thing? Well, they *can* be but it's up to you in regards to the light you shine upon them, what you get from them, and how committed you are to rectifying a mistake.

Here's the thing though, there are several types of mistakes we can commit and understand each a bit better can help you cope with them or respond to them better.

1. Not Knowing. Committing a mistake because you didn't know something is actually quite common. The easiest way to rectify this is to learn. People might laugh because you didn't know, but after you learn, they'll eventually look foolish if they keep laughing at something you learned how to move past.

2. Presuming. A lot of people think they know exactly how to do things and execute, because they thought they knew how something needed to be done. In my experience, presuming is the easiest way to commit a mistake. The antidote to this is clarifying. If you're not sure, ask. If you're not clear, clarify. Not doing this means you're taking a risk in regards to what has to be done. And guess what, sometimes time is of the essence so clarifying can actually be the best thing you can do.

3. Learning incorrectly. Sometimes people in positions of power teach us things that are wrong or teach us things that can be improved. In fact, in some instances, everyone agrees on certain information set forth by paradigms only to be corrected by someone who finds evidence that disproves established knowledge. Lest we forget, the world was once flat and a proton was once the smallest particle known to man. Now we know better and here the trick is to be flexible and objective in regards to information. It's not to say that you should jump towards any new theory, but you should hear it out and if something seems plausible, study it if only to accept the possibility of something. As humans, we're addicted to order and what many people call "the truth." The fact is that the truth is as elusive as order. There may be amazing laws of physics occurring constantly throughout the universe, but the level of controlled chaos we witness every second should serve as a reminder that there is no such thing as permanent order. If you don't agree with this, then, by all means, explain earthquakes, hurricanes, tornadoes, floods, eruptions, volcanos, tsunamis, and the such. Order is something we wish and strive for, but by learning, we can better handle the chaos we truly live in.

4. Bad execution. Sometimes we know what to do and how to do it, but we still botch it. As we mentioned before, we're human and mistakes do happen. The way to minimize these types of mistakes is to practice. It sounds clichéd and almost hackneyed but the truth of the matter is that our bodies are often smarter than our brains and muscle memory and instinct can go a long way to avoiding all sorts of mistakes.

Like these, it's probable that we can find plenty more examples because mistakes are an inherent part of existence. If we blame someone else for our mistake, then it's a waste of time. Actually, it's twice as much of a waste if it's truly your mistake. Think about it. If you commit a mistake and rectify it, that's one response you had to give. However, if you commit a mistake and blame someone else, you need to blame someone else, convince them that it wasn't your mistake, reinforce that it wasn't a mistake, possibly look for a solution while still maintaining your innocence, and then you have to remember what the lie was to ensure it never stains your reputation. If you ask me, that does sound like way too much effort instead of simply fixing the mistake, but hey, it's your life and your call. Like I said before, I do my best to not judge. I won't say you're doing it wrong, but also will not waste one second on calling you on your mistake. The fact is, the faster we sort what happened, the easier it is to remedy it.

RETURN OF INVESTMENT

In the past, I've been called hard to work with and hot-tempered for varying reasons. I can justify either of these claims or I may accept that I could make things better by sharing my part of the blame and being accountable. I've done that for years and the result is that when I say something, people listen to me and if I commit a mistake, it gets fixed as fast as humanly possible. This in part has rewarded me with the respect of several people I've worked with, because although I'm not perfect, they know I'll do whatever needs to be done so we can all accomplish established goals. This, in turn, has taught me that there is a LOT to be received by always being accountable for your actions.

1. PEOPLE WILL BELIEVE YOU

Some people cry wolf and eventually, others stop believing what they are saying. When you are accountable and do things you say will do, hand in things on the date that you said you will, admit to mistakes committed and rectify them, or make sure you always deliver, that tells people that when you say something, it's the truth and that what you say you mean.

2. YOU SAVE TIME

Accountability always helps save time instead of the alternative. You don't waste any energy on lying or covering your tracks. You fess up, rectify, and do what you have to do. No dillying or dallying, only doing.

3. YOU GET HEARD

If you are someone people can trust, so can your ideas and opinions. This is something you have to earn, but it's worth every single effort. I know full well the difference of having my opinion valued and having it not be taken into consideration and guess what, you don't need to pander or kiss ass to achieve this. All you need to do is deliver on what you promise.

4. YOU ARE GIVEN OPPORTUNITIES

It doesn't matter the context, if you are accountable for what you promise, life will continue to give you opportunities. If you're a writer and promise a great book, delivering on it will get more people to read you. If you say a dish on your menu changes lives and in fact, it's THAT amazing, people will flock to your restaurant. If you say your results as a physician are guaranteed and they are, the waiting list for your services will be long.

SUMMARY AND TIPS:

Accountability goes a long way to making life easier and richer. It avoids you needing to spend unnecessary time, energy, and resources to cover up a mistake and instead allows you to learn and to be respected by others.

The main tips I can offer are as follows:
- If you have a fault, try to improve on it
- If you commit a mistake, admit to it and correct it as fast as humanly possible
- Learn from your mistakes
- Rise above your faults and mistakes
- Deliver what you promise
- Meet or exceed expectations
- Learn from your mistakes (worth mentioning twice)

Chapter 13:
Do good, damn it

Let's say it again, in CAPS, **bold**, and <u>underlined</u>:

<u>DO GOOD, DAMN IT</u>

For your enjoyment, I even increased the font size from 11 points to 16 because it's something that I believe should be repeated and shouted in every corner of the world. Are there crappy people? Yes. Are there vile people and criminals? Yes. Is there corruption? Yes. Is there injustice? Yes. Do bad things happen to good people? Of course they do. And guess what? ALL of these are further reasons to do good, damn it.

You can do good every single day. You can make it your life quest and you can change the world because change comes about through action and sometimes action can be a huge thing and sometimes for that huge thing to happen, you need to do a small thing first.

DON'T SETTLE FOR THINKING, DO!

Too often we fall into the trap of thinking about all the good things we can do and somehow we don't get around to doing them. It's an odd sort of behavior, but it's a lot more common than you think. That's because we think about doing good, we worry about good, we even plan for doing good, but if it's not perfect, we hold off from doing it. This begs the question, does half the good you had in mind still not represent good? Does half an effort still make a difference?

Too often we obsess about details and perfection. We have this perfect movie scene in our head of all the good we want to do, but to do it *that* way, we need to do X, Y, Z, Ω, α, and π. The level of planning we want to do can limit what we actually do, but that's only part of it. We've mentioned before that thinking about doing good is actually comforting for people, because they thought about it. You know, thoughts and prayers and all that jazz. But good needs to be *done*, not just thought of, not simply felt, not only wished upon, it must be done and done to the capacity that we can do it.

You want to send $300 worth of aid but can only afford $75? Send the $75. You don't need to tell anyone you wanted to send $300 and someone really has to tell you that. You give what you want to or what you can and it's not a matter of it being enough or not, it's a matter of actually giving and doing something and not limiting yourself to theorizing, planning, or fantasizing about all the good you can do.

The mind is an incredible thing and should be the most powerful muscle in our body because it has so many functions to it. But the mind can distract us from carrying out an action.

"I wish I could do more."

"I'll make sure to do something next Tuesday."

"Maybe later."

There is a lot of danger in the word *later* because so often in our lives, later never comes. We push later so far off into the future that we can't even see it, or we keep pushing it off just enough so that our conscience is at ease. I for one would like to tell you to NOT be at ease. Don't settle for thinking about something. Do it. And if it's something good that can help someone else, then what the hell are you waiting for?

Need information to do the thing? Search it out.

Need help to do the thing? Ask for it.

Need a ride to do the thing? Find out what options you have.

But do something.

Why do I say this? Because as time passes by, you lose those opportunities to help. You settle. You become static. You forget the power in your life that doing good can bring, for others, but for you as well.

I've known to take a bad day and turn it around completely by doing a series of good acts. It needn't be something huge but it allows me to switch gears. It also shows that I am much more in control of what I do in this life and that within my power there is a lot of good I can do, even when I'm short on money, time, or energy.

Unfortunately, a lot of people play the wishful thinking game and then they even wonder why they don't get thanked for anything. Well, it's pretty simple: if you have the intention of doing something but don't actually do anything, then what is it that people should be thankful for? You see, intention is a wonderful thing, but it lives in the same realm as thoughts and prayers. It's in the ether and it's a beautiful shining thing, but if you don't pull it into reality through action, then it's a pipe dream, it's ethereal to the point that it's nothing.

Creative kindness has been talked about in several instances in this book but in no other chapter shall it be called for more adamantly than in this one. That's because creative kindness demands that you act those times you have a good intention. It can be some times, most times, or all the time, but it **demands** action.

If you have an inkling of an idea to help someone, you do it. You see someone hungry, you listen to that voice that wonders if the person has had something to eat and you ignore the voices that distract you from doing good. There are people in dire situations that you know nothing about. Right now there are people who were extremely successful in their field at one time in their lives and something happened and now they don't even have a roof over their head.

But it's not just homeless people I'm talking about. Creative kindness knows no limits except the ones you establish on it. If you see someone being bullied, creative kindness can help you intervene in so many ways that it baffles the mind, but if all you do is feel bad for the person being bullied, then guess what, intention was good for nothing and the person shall continue to get bullied. Do you know someone who has a dream of being X or Y thing? Then help them. I've known to revise cover letters, résumés, query letters, help people practice for interviews, offered advice on writing, on life, on health, on anything, because if I see a person with a situation and I have the means to help in any way, for however small it can be, I want to have the peace of mind that I've acted more than I've thought about it.

Thinking about things is nice, it's fun even, but it doesn't do anything. Want a perfect example? I'm a writer, but if all I do is plot an outline, research, and investigate, the words do not get written and the stories stay in my mind. My action there is to put a pen in my hand or put my fingers on the keyboard and go with it. Action. Executing the idea I have in mind. Do you know why I offered this example? Because I've lost count of the amount of times I've heard people tell me they have a great idea. The problem is that in some cases, years pass and the person has still not written one word.

Another example of creative kindness can be one of my projects I've titled *Blanc Comics*. After hearing many aspiring artists who don't have a forum to show their talents, I did an entire series called *Blanc Comics* where I write the plot, design the panels, give instructions of what should appear in the panels and have done 8 different volumes. It's in part a tribute to my grandmother who had glaucoma and in part to help aspiring artists. Do you know how many complete volumes I've seen? None. But I continue to promote it in the hopes that it helps artists go for it. They can put it in their portfolio and if they want to say we did a collaboration, they can and should if it helps their cause.

Like this, there are countless examples of things people say they want to do yet somehow put off for years upon years, even if it's for their benefit. They relish in the comfort of the desire to do something but stay there, lingering and idle, and convincing themselves of the value of the word *soon.* Soon is another one of those dangerous terms that if you're not accountable AND careful it can eat up ALL your time and leave you nothing in return. Soon is a toxic myth you need to redefine, if this is your case.

Alas, people invest in *soon* and *later* all too often, forgetting that **now** is the only moment when you can live and have a real impact.

RETURN OF INVESTMENT

Doing good is something everyone can do and there are millions of ways where we can do good. We just need to either do it or be creative in regards to how we do it. But most importantly, we need to do it, not merely settle for thinking about it. Although the reasons why doing good are plenty varied, here are 4 for you.

1. DOING INSTEAD OF THINKING FEELS GREAT

Any and every one can dream, but not everyone actually gets to do what they think about. When it comes to good, doing means that whatever you thought actually came true, which is a very empowering thing to do good and to also do the things you want to do in life. We watch so many movies and read so many stories that sometimes we forget that we can be the protagonist of a real life story. That's the power of *doing* over *thinking about doing*. When you see that what was in your mind can be real, there are no limits to what you can do.

2. DOING MEANS YOU CAN DO MORE

We all have countless dreams and things we want to do. Once we do one, we see that more things are possible and the more we do the more empowered we become. When you do something, that makes whatever you thought of real. This can have a profound effect on your life and the things you've always said you wanted to do but hadn't done yet, for whatever the reason. That's because action inspires. And when I say inspires, I mean others AND yourself.

3. YOU CAN INSPIRE OTHERS

Let it be clear, doing good is rarely a one-off sort of thing. When you do good, others take note and often take action. That means you can be a catalyst for others. So much good can come from your actions and all you have to do is allow yourself to unleash good on the world. Kindness has a way of rippling throughout the world and in these times, where a friend can live next door or on the other side of the planet, there's no telling how much your good actions can inspire or how far your inspiration and motivation can reach.

4. DOING GOOD IS GOOD FOR YOU

It is clinically proven that doing acts of kindness is good for the mind, the soul, and literally the heart. You have more energy. You sleep better. It promotes wellness that increases lifespans. Medical outcomes improve. You get sick less. The benefits of kindness far outweigh the weight of limiting yourself to thinking about it, so by all means, have at it and feel good about it.

SUMMARY AND TIPS:

Kindness is a powerful thing that can change the world. I truly believe that the world needs more kindness in as many expressions as we can find. Kindness needs to come out of our thoughts and dreams and flood the real world. Kindness to others. Kindness to the environment. Kindness to our fellow humans regardless of the color of their skin or the language or their religion.

But kindness needs action. Kindness begs to be released in the now more than it needs to be planned for the future. We are great at finding excuses and we need to get worse at that skill and way better at going with the flow of our soul and doing good just for the sake of doing good. If you think you can do something, then do it. Don't perfect it, do it. Do what you can and if you feel like you want to do more later, then do more. There's nothing wrong with that.

Creativity can help with bringing about kindness and there's no limit to how many ways it can be expressed. The opposite is actually true. Kindness knows no limits unless you put them on whatever you think of.

There are a lot of people who need help in this world, who need food or shelter or a kind ear to talk. You can be the action of kindness and you can bring it but you have to do, not think, not wish, not wonder, DO.

So let's say it again, CAPS, **bold**, and <u>underlined:</u>

<u>DO GOOD DAMN IT</u>

Chapter 14:
Don't waste creativity
on excuses

Excuses are a waste of time, energy, creativity, and calories.

If it's not extremely clear from the first sentence above, I'm not a fan of excuses. Actually, a lot of people aren't a fan of excuses although one small tidbit definitely must be clarified; people aren't fans of excuses when they are being *given* the excuse for one situation or another. It's a whole other matter when it comes to them having to justify something that they did or didn't do. In that case, of COURSE an exception should apply and be accepted. After all, it's not that they're giving an excuse, because *of course* they aren't.

The first thing about excuses is the need to accept that at one point or another, we give them. It's a completely normal reaction and we need to know when and why we give an excuse. Sometimes things really are outside our control, and in those times, it's definitely a great idea to come clean. But many times we could have avoided a situation entirely and that's something a lot of people have a hard time of accepting. That's because it all comes back to accountability. If you constantly deliver, people will listen to what you have to say and believe the reasons you give for doing or not doing something. But if you constantly have an excuse, every single time, then of course it's only natural that everything becomes suspect. Not only that, but some stories a few people give are so intensely lavish that you wonder why they don't pursue a career in writing or acting.

There's also another detail, some people forget that the truth is out there. If you give a valid excuse, then that's fine. You won't need to fabricate evidence or find willing "witnesses" to lie, if need be. Life happens and weird things most definitely happen every single day. Cars don't start, traffic can be and often is absolutely bonkers, and yes, dogs do sometimes eat your homework.

It's funny because the dog eating homework bit is naturally understood as being a blatant lie to get out of handing in work. The reason I find it so funny is because on two occasions my dogs really *did* chew up my homework. Knowing full well I wouldn't be believed, I brought the tattered homework to show that I was in fact telling the truth (Funny side note: on one occasion it was chewed up; but on another occasion, it was another deed done by the dog. Although we can possibly debate whether my dog hated that project as much as I did, what we can't debate is that the end result was quite... *colorful?* And if you're wondering, yes I did take the work in a Ziploc bag as evidence.)

So what's the point? I learned that giving an excuse is completely acceptable especially when you offer proactive alternatives. There's a big difference between standing there with no options expecting a hand out or being absolved of any responsibility and it's a whole other thing when you say something like, "I need this amount of time to deliver the work and my apologies for this, I understand if you need to take credit off my grade, although I'll do my best to make up for it." I once knew to tell a teacher that I understood if I couldn't be allowed to hand in the paper but that I would still do it, because it was the principle of the matter and I didn't want them to think I was slacking and merely doing my best to avoid doing the work. Fortunately, the professor saw the commitment in me and allowed me to hand it in two days later, but told me that I couldn't get more than a B. And a B I got. It would have been an A on paper, and we both knew it, but that's the thing, knowing the worth of my work was more important than my actual grade.

Being proactive while showing you care and that you want to be responsible goes a LONG way in offering you second chances, alternatives, and getting people to accept if you happen to not deliver what you said you would when you would, because it's an exception or an anomaly, not the norm. Going above and beyond your initial effort will also go a long way to getting you back in the graces of someone. Think about it, not handing something in can and does happen. It's not the end of the world but we really shouldn't treat it lightly either. If when you finally do get to hand in something that's already late, you hand something that's either subpar or merely meets the bare minimum, how do you think that will go down? If instead you hand in something that FAR exceeds expectations, what type of reaction do you think it will receive? How do you think you will feel as well?

Now going back to the excuse, valid or not, the less time you spend on it, the better. Some people invest more time on an excuse than they do on the work or the things they have to do. They plan, embellish, construct, and perfect the excuse so that it's foolproof. Then when they deliver it, they realize that all the work that they had done was for not because they *still* have to do the other work. Again, life happens, and that's fine and dandy, but a good excuse doesn't excuse you from the things you have to do in life.

Here's the thing: excuses come in many shapes and sizes and sometimes there's an event and you don't want to go to it, so you bail. Maybe you had to call someone and didn't. Maybe you had to write someone and didn't either. The number of scenarios we can think of are boundless, but in each you have the option of coming clean or having to not only come up with an excuse, but remember it for as long as you live. OK, maybe it's not that drastic, but it is rather a lot of hassle instead of saying "thanks, but no thanks." But that's the thing, we hate to disappoint, so we'd rather avoid the truth to avoid confrontation in regards to something we might or might not be right in our assessment. And in today's world, it's even more fun because it means you can't post any pictures of anything you did in the time allotted for the event that you "couldn't make it to."

The sad reality is that we often look for excuses to not do things and can be wildly creative in finding ways of not only **not** doing something, but of justifying said inaction, while still managing to feel bad we didn't do it. It's not to say we have to do everything we're offered, but I do wonder how some people would feel if instead of an excuse to *not* do something, they found a reason to actually *do* something.

Imagine the impact that shift of perspective could have, especially because odds are we all know someone who always finds a reason not to do something but rarely finds a reason to do something. There's the illusion of control or even safety, but dig a bit further and there's also disappointment to be found.

This can go for so many things in life, even being in touch with people. The number of reasons that can be found to not call, text, or write someone is endless and when you look at them objectively, most if any don't make much sense. But taking that step is such a difficult thing for so many of us. We think. We rethink. We think some more. We overthink. And still we think some more. Then you finally get in touch and it's awkward when the inevitable question pops its head, "why didn't you call or write?" It's crazy because if there's anything that is completely doable in this life, it's staying in touch, which shows that many of us are actually pretty bad at it. A lot of it can come down to ego (why don't they write or call and I have to be the one to do so?) but more often than it's normal to report, people feel like they're too busy, or they'll do it later, or not right now, but soon. That word again... *soon.* It robs us of so many good times and great experiences with the false notion of nearness.

RETURN OF INVESTMENT

Excuses limit how much we live, experience, and enjoy. It's a mechanism that doesn't make much sense because it can feed a variety of feelings of malaise in any given person, yet we do it. And we do it a lot. And there's plenty of reasons why we should find more reasons and less excuses, but here's four to try on for size.

1. TIME WELL SPENT

If you don't spend time on developing, giving, and justifying excuses, you have more time for things that do matter. Excuses are a time and energy waster so the less you give the less you lose.

2. SIMPLIFIED LIFE

Keeping track of excuses is one part of this equation, but the other part is more practical. If you have to give an excuse and substantiate it and constantly defend it, that's a lot of effort instead of doing what you have to do. It's the difference between doing one action and doing five or more.

3. AVOID HAVING TO GO INTO WITNESS PROTECTION

The level of complexity of some excuses could win the person a Nobel prize in literature for the sheer elaborateness of the story. Also, if you're playing hooky or even avoiding someone, you have to probably modify a ton of things you're doing or will do to ensure you're not caught. It almost begs the question "is it worth it?" But no doubt some people get a thrill out of having to hide out and limit themselves to "stick it to the man". In the end, if it's something that offers you a thrill, then have it, but it definitely seems like there are better options of things to do with your time and energy.

4. YOU FOCUS ON WHAT MATTERS

When you focus on getting things done, that's all there is. Apart from a waste of time and energy, excuses distract you from your goals and the things you need to do or the things that make you happy. Focus is one of the best skills to hone. So the choice is clear, hone and sharpen that focus or dull it with excuses. It's not much of a choice, but in the end, we all have decisions to make and lives to live.

SUMMARY AND TIPS:

Excuses aren't always a bad thing, but they can't be your go-to solution for situations if you want to be successful, happy, and have peace of mind. They serve their purpose the more sparingly you use them and become a hindrance and a chore the more you do. They can also be used for many things in life and can even convince you of a point of view that isn't necessarily the truth but is more comfortable than the truth.

Accountability goes a long way to make sure you don't need to use excuses as much. And when you do, they don't even come off as excuses, they come off as a valid reason for something that did or didn't get done.

If you find yourself overwhelmed by excuses, sometimes it's best to come clean and the best option is to avoid them.

Does it mean extra effort? Well not really. An excuse and justifying it is extra effort personified in and of itself. It means that you have to worry about the thing you have to do plus the reasons why you haven't done it and justifying it. So if you feel yourself about to give an excuse, don't. If you find yourself looking for a reason not to do something, switch it up and find a reason to do something. In the end, it'll be a better use of time and by only focusing what matters, you'll have time to spare.

Chapter 15:
Manners can
change the world

People underestimate the value and power of manners. How do I know this? Because every time I show manners, people are surprised.

Manners are a peculiar thing and something that changes from one country to the next. It's not a consistent set of values, but many of them do share common ground. Here's one small example: in the US, proper manners dictate you should pinch the fork with the left hand, cut with the right hand, and switch. In Europe, you don't switch hands. Another example, I was taught that to be courteous, a man should walk on the outside of a woman while walking down the street because she's not for sale. In other cultures, the man walks on the inside because people in apartments would toss buckets of water (or things much less savory than water) either out the door or the window. So to avoid ruining a dress and tarnishing a woman's dignity, a man would take the hit, in theory.

As you can see, what changes are the things you're taught. What doesn't change is that you're trying to think of others and maintaining manners. Even so, there are other things that are good manners that can and do change the world.

GREETINGS FELLOW HUMAN

A good morning, good afternoon, and good evening is something we should always give and give freely. But that isn't the case with people. How often have you stepped into an elevator where everyone seems to be intent on listening to themselves breathe? It's something small but it's something a lot of people have lost, which is a shame. I do my best to say good morning, good afternoon, good evening, or any variation of 'hello' if only to show that I recognize the existence of other humans.

Human contact is a curious thing, especially nowadays. 'We text and tweet up a storm and do an amazing job of staying in touch, but when it comes to direct contact with other humans who actually inhabit your immediate vicinity, things get weird. It could be partly the times we live in, but that's being lazy, putting the blame on "the times."

I think that although this comes down in part to where you live in, places where people would be ultra-friendly have shut themselves off from the rest of the world, for whatever the reason. Although I can understand this, I've definitely learned that a greeting can actually improve the chances of people helping you or making them more receptive to your existence in general.

Since I'm so fond of them, here's some real life examples I can share:

- **TECH SUPPORT**: By consistently saying good morning and going out of my way to say hi to people in the accounting and IT departments, if ever I had a situation, they always made sure I had a prompt solution. I didn't do it to butter them up though, and I do feel the need to clarify. I went to say hello and asked them about life because these people ALWAYS get calls when someone either has a problem or need something. So imagine their surprise when someone actually cares about them. By caring, by saying hi, by appreciating and giving them good reviews through whatever mechanism I could have at my disposal, I made sure that our relationship was ALWAYS positive. That goes a long way to help your life be easier, and it all started with a hello.

- **EXTRA SERVINGS**: I once did an internship in NYC and from here I realized how rare it is for some people to be treated friendly. On one side, I always said hello to cafeteria personnel in the building cafeteria. I struck small talk that lasted anywhere from 40 seconds to 2 minutes but that made a difference. They saw me and smiled while giving me an extra slice of beef/turkey/or chicken. There was also a quaint cafeteria near the dorm where I stayed that was run by some wonderful Dominican people. If you didn't know, the Dominican Republic and Puerto Rico are neighbors in the Caribbean. For some extra insight, know that DR and PR have several rivalries in sports and life that quite honestly, don't make sense. To put it succinctly, Puerto Ricans are often not that fond of Dominicans and vice versa. For me, I see them as neighbors and friendly ones at that and the nicest Hispanic people I came into contact in NYC were by far the Dominicans. The woman who cut my hair was Dominican and that restaurant had the best *comida criolla (typical*

Caribbean food fare). By saying hi, *buenos días,* and being nice to them, they always took care of me. They would say: "Mijo, you're too skinny," and serve me an extra pork chop or more rice or more salad and in return, I would leave a good tip even if I was a student. They insisted I didn't have to but I felt the need to do so, and I could, so I did. These two examples are of Hispanics, but in one example, they were mainly Mexicans and in another they were Dominicans and I use these two examples to show that some of the divides we have due to where we grow up make no sense and need not apply to being nice to people.

- **CLEANEST AREA**: I always make it a point to say hello, thank you, and interact with people who work in maintenance. The reason is that people have a way of treating the people that deal with their garbage as if they don't matter, or worse yet, as if they were garbage. It's not just that I don't get this type of behavior, it's that I detest it. So throughout the years, some of the people I've been the nicest to are from maintenance, because they are SO essential to a pleasant work environment. The fact is that most people are sloppy and messy. If it weren't for maintenance personnel, we'd work in pigsties because we're special like that. For some reason, people forget that maintenance personnel are people as well. It's not only a myopic way of seeing life, it's also a bit on the mean side. By being nice to maintenance personnel, which goes from saying hi, asking about their family and going up to offering them a ride, my work areas were always clean and if I needed help with something, the answer was always yes.

The lesson here is simple: don't take anyone for granted. On the one hand, you never know whose help you'll need one day. And for another thing, it's basic respect for your fellow human.

PLEASE AND THANK YOU

That we need to be reminded of the value of *please* and *thank you* should be an embarrassment to us as a species, but that's the reality we live in. When people order their food, they say "bring me this or that." For me, I value saying something more along the lines of "good afternoon, may I please have this or that item." After they write down the order, I say thank you and I also make it a thing to say thank you every time they refill my water and bring or take away my plates. I know it's part of their job, but I know what it's like to have a parched throat and nothing to drink and I know what it's like to have a table full of dirty dishes. So it's only natural to tell them thanks for a job well done.

Unfortunately, we live in a "time is money" period in history where people think that saying thank you and please are a waste of time. They'd rather be expedient than waste time on pleasantries. That's their right to do so and hooray for not being nice to the person who will bring you the food you're going to eat. Karma is a thing but some people also recognize that rude people deserve rude treatment, especially because there's no reason to deliver or receive rude treatment. I know there's no reason to be nice either, but if you have a choice, why go with the one that makes you look like an ass and unpleasant to deal with?

Please and thank you should be in the cornerstone of your vocabulary because they are words that demonstrate that you actually value a person's time and what they do. Please and thank you are also things that motivate... you and other people. At least in my case, when someone is exceptionally courteous, it inspires me to bring my A-game, which is why I offer that to people whom I come in contact with. Will that guarantee that you won't find rude people? Not at all, but it's up to you how you act and react to what life brings your way.

HOORAY FOR FREE STUFF

Want another added incentive to practice good manners? You can get free upgrades and goodies from time to time. How, you may ask. Simple, imagine this scenario: you are in a queue at some place, let's say a fast food restaurant. In front of you is a character that is unpleasant to say the least. They're rude, treat the server like crap, some might even yell at them. They either stomp down the line after they place their order or they can even storm off. Seeing this situation, the person at the register is already compromised, meaning that they are possibly emotionally affected, because who likes that kind of treatment.

So you're up, you can either downplay it and be very courteous and kind or actually check to see how they are. I've actually done both because you can have an idea from a person's body language if they're receptive to kindness or need a minute. I've told the cashier, "hi there," and either crack a joke or ask if they're OK. I make sure to always say please and when they've taken my order, I say thank you and that I hope their day gets better and better. This type of approach has gained me extra fries, an upgraded soda, an extra biscuit, but more than that, it's allowed me to make a difference in the day of someone who isn't having an easy time. I've been thanked for the kindness and on occasions where I've gone back to the place, I get a hello and an extra thank you for what I did or said the other day. It's a small gesture but it makes a BIG difference and it's the type of thing that is nice to have it follow you around.

A REACTION GETS A REACTION

It's not farfetched to imagine that if you're always rude, always obnoxious, and always cranky, then people will take you as you are and never notice if there's something truly wrong with you. If by contrast, you are always courteous and kind and have a reaction, people notice quite a lot. If you're a regular in a restaurant and have a reaction like that, trust me, someone will intervene. If you're at your job and have a reaction, rather than putting you down, people will ask what happened and try and help you sort it. The question is, which one do you want to be? There's no right or wrong answer, which goes back to accountability, but for me, if I have a situation and actually have an outburst, I don't mind people cutting me some slack just because that's not the way I usually am. Imagine the flipside. If you're always cranky, getting help becomes that much harder and I don't say that from a speculative point of view, I say that because once upon a time, I was cynical and could easily get in a bad mood. It's all very much like the tale of the boy who cried wolf.

GLOBAL MANNERS

Take a brief look at what we've discussed in this chapter. Now imagine if we applied them on a global scale. Imagine if in the murky world of politics manners were practiced more than political correctness. I know it's a stretch, but if we can imagine whole new worlds and galaxies populated by all sorts of inhabitants, there's no reason to deprive ourselves of the ability to dream of a world where people were nicer. Sure, there'd be disagreements on which hand to use to cut your food, but it'd be better.

Instead, we live in a world of shoving matches, a world of imposing agendas and ideologies, of intolerance and bigotry. And lest you think otherwise, bigotry and misogyny have in common that they are both two types of behavior deeply embedded in rudeness. Being impolite to someone because of their gender, sexual preference, race, skin color, age, social caste, or medical condition has a firm base on being rude, on thinking someone isn't as good as you, on demeaning others. More than being based on feeling superior to others, manners are meant to show we care about how we interact with others and are considerate under several types of circumstances.

But I really do believe manners can change the world and not just in human interactions, but the world in general. Good manners dictate that you should be tidy which can easily be transferred to recycling and business practices that aren't detrimental to the environment. It means picking up after yourself and others. It means helping rather than hindering. It can mean so many things and none of them are bad.

RETURN OF INVESTMENT

Some people think having good manners is old school. I have no problem with that because I am old school and think that some of the best lessons I've learned in life come from being old school. As for you, here are four reasons why you should have good manners or keep improving on yours.

1. PEOPLE ARE MORE LIKELY TO HELP YOU

It's been mentioned before in the chapter but I'll repeat it for your benefit. If you're nice and have good manners, people will be more likely to help you than if you're rude or lack manners. Firstly, they take you more seriously.

Secondly, they're so surprised by good manners that they really go above and beyond to make sure you're OK.

2. IT CAN VASTLY IMPROVE SOMEONE'S DAY

If someone is dealing with crappy people ALL day, you will be someone's angel. You will be their respite. You will keep them from having a complete meltdown. If it sounds drastic, well sometimes it is. If someone right before you behaves rudely, you have the opportunity to be a positive in that person's day. All of us want our worth recognized and some appreciation and good manners go a long way to making a huge difference for people who aren't having the best of days.

3. IT IS AN ASSET

Having good manners is good for business and great for your career. Although some people can get away with being assholes, a lot of successful people are actually quite courteous and have fantastic manners. That's because you never know in what context you'll be in and being prepared for anything is the best option, whether you're tossed into a rib fest, or invited to a royal dinner. Also, older people respond to manners and having manners and knowing how to behave means that people can count on being able to send you to any meeting with any client because you'll always behave.

4. IT CAN CHANGE THE WORLD FOR THE BETTER

A lot of conflicts in this world could probably be avoided if we all practiced better manners. Regardless of what goes on in the world, giving our best is always an option and often the best option at that. If you have manners, positive resolutions are easier to come by than if you're rude and obnoxious. If instead you are level headed and always maintain composure, that means you maintain control and any slight will make the other party look bad. So stay in control and show the world that being classy is good for the world.

SUMMARY AND TIPS:

Manners are in certain circles almost a lost art form in and of itself and it doesn't have to be that way. It's not merely about making older people smile at someone still having manners, it's just a better way to live and get along with people.

If you're ever at a loss in regards to manners, then by all means, ask and search. The Internet is full of information and if you want to learn about manners, there's probably an app, a tutorial, or a website for that.

Practicing good manners is also often good for your health. If you think about the slicing food and switching hands, that definitely forces you to eat slower and savor the meal. Not only that, it gives you the opportunity to chew properly. So look for all the positives that can come from having good manners. Who knows? Great things might just come your way.

Chapter 16: Define yourself

Who you are shall forever be up to you and ONLY you.

A lot of people use crutches to justify aspects of who and how they are. I was born in this place, so of course I should be this way. I'm a Libra, so obviously what I did was logical behavior for someone born under this astrological sign. Since I'm Hispanic, X or Y come naturally to me and it's not something I can change... ever.

Excuses. That's what these things are. We've talked about excuses and how they're a waste of time. Life isn't some scenario where you have no say in what happens to you. Your circumstances might be influenced by where you come from and certain aspects may actually be out of your control, but for the most part, where you are is in part due to how you are... and some people don't like to hear that for however true it is. And guess what? It's plenty true.

It's up to you to define who you are. A lot of people want to say that they do, but peer pressure is fun like that, making people do things they wouldn't normally do but they end up justifying their behavior because after all, that's the "normal" and "common" thing to do. The reality is that caving in to fashion, trends, fads, and peer pressure all respond to that part of us that seeks for and craves acceptance. It's not so much that it's a bad thing, it's more that people keep forgetting how much control they have in regards to how they live life.

TEMP CONTROL

Human behavior might be highly susceptible to influence

and suggestion, but that doesn't mean we don't have control. One's temper is the responsibility of one person and that person looks back at you every time you stare into a mirror.

For the longest time, I've been known to be explosive, have a temper, and even be grumpy. It's a reputation I earned by how I reacted to certain things and regardless of how justified or not I was in my reactions, the reactions were mine and mine alone. It's taken years to shift my mentality from pessimist to optimist and to know my triggers and trigger warnings to learn how to keep myself in check, but fortunately I have. Nowadays, it takes either a LOT more to elicit a temper-filled reaction or something related to specific topics and every day I work hard to bring forth a better version of me. A calmer more mature version and trust me it's a LOT of work. Not only that but it's also a lot of work that goes unrecognized. Earn a reputation and shaking it off will take a LOT of effort, but it is possible and you're not bound to it for life. It's just that you won't get a medal for becoming a better version of you.

The main thing is that what I do, I do for myself. The perception of my temper might have been well earned, but it was external. How I felt about that perception and what I could do to improve it was all well within my control and all it takes is time and effort and if something is worthwhile, that's a ridiculously low price to pay.

The fact of the matter is that how you behave is ALL in your court. The world has rude people. The world has bad people. Life has unjust situations. That is all out there and there's not much you can do about what's out there. But how you react and how you behave in general is all on you.

Holding a grudge is a full on decision and a draining one at that. That said, a LOT of people act as if they don't have a choice BUT to hold that grudge.

It's the principle of the matter.

It was wrong.

They don't deserve forgiveness or a second chance.

There's plenty of ways to react... but in the end it's all a decision on your side of the court. The more I live the less I want to hold grudges. Not because I'm not capable of doing so, but because it is so draining and in large part, you're allowing other people and how they make you feel define how you behave. NO one should have that much power over you in this life, but unfortunately they do. Some people might want to justify a grudge, but in the end, holding a grudge is harder than letting it go and I know this from experience.

For the longest time, I held one or two grudges against people I REALLY didn't like. If they would go to some place, I'd try to get out of that event. If we had friends in common, I'd hang out less with some or I'd ask if the person I didn't like would be there. Again, that's WAY too much power I used to give some people over my life and how I lived it. That my reactions were visceral could be easily understood thanks to one douche comment one guy said trying to be mister funny man, some heartbreak I endured, or some other event that got people black listed in my life. For the longest time I saw one guy and was honestly tempted to let go and have a proper fight. For the longest time, I said mean things about some people because they had "wronged me." It was to that level, but I mainly festered and fumed and then one day I realized what a waste of time those grudges were. That's because the entire existence of these people isn't meant as a spite against me and some people are simply not your cup of tea, to put it lightly, and full on assholes that aren't worth your time if you want a statement with a little more bite to it. It's not like I love the guy now or think constantly of the other people, but I honestly don't waste one calorie or one second thinking about them because nothing good will come from it.

This hasn't happened many times in my life, but in our time on this little place we call Earth some people will either wrong you or hurt you or something else and however much you want to give of your energy to dedicate to being pissed off at them is your decision. Slowly but surely, I've decided I want to limit or nullify any and all energetic investments in said people. A grudge and spite are crosses we carry and if we don't let them go, we can carry them for a LONG time. Trust me, I carried several for years until bit by bit I got tired of being angry with people. So I let go of one grudge, and it felt great. So I've let go of most if not all of them and it's the lightest I've ever felt. I no longer waste my time on things like that and instead invest it in WAY better things, like helping others, writing stories/poetry/music, or creating. In the end, it's been my choice, and I'm endlessly happy with it.

LIKE WHAT YOU LIKE

The amount of energy people spend on appeasing to the likes of other people is scary. I could say it's ridiculous or crazy, but it's not. There's actually a simple reason behind such behavior. People want to be accepted, so they learn to like what other people like and hate what other people hate. It's nice to have company, but it's a disingenuous way of life.

That's why I always say "like what you like." Don't justify, don't defend. Just be you and do you. Do you like the color purple? Rock it. Are you a fan of a band EVERYBODY hates? Their loss. Do you hate a book everyone raves about? Then stick to your guns and define what you enjoy based EXCLUSIVELY on what your experience is. After all, it is your bookshelf. So put whatever you like on it. There's no need for any of us to actively pursue homogeneity and that would actually be one of the worst things we can achieve or even strive for.

Want some examples? Here's a couple.

My favorite bands are Pearl Jam, Elbow, Soundgarden, Blind Melon, Alice in Chains, Tool, Nine Inch Nails, Radiohead, and the list goes on and on. Did I mention the Beatles and The Rolling Stones? Nope. And it's not because I don't appreciate them or recognize their significance, impact, or legacies; it's because the bands I mentioned have been an integral part of my life and have helped me define part of who I am. Do I like Nickelback and Creed? No I don't, but that doesn't mean I don't enjoy some tracks from them, most notably off their wayyyyy older records. Is that me caving in to public opinion? Not at all. That's me stating facts. I adore Tori Amos and Ani Di Franco and I say so proudly, not because I want to impress anyone who is a fan, but because I honestly adore their music.

The same goes for movies. People rave about *Avatar* and *Rosemary's Baby*. In my life, they are as irrelevant as a toilet catalog in the best of times and both experiences left me short changed at best. I think they are over hyped, poorly scripted, poorly acted films regardless of whatever accolades they are given or status as American Classics. That's because I choose to have my own opinion over the things I watch. For the same part, John Carpenter's *Big Trouble In Little China*, which was originally shunned by critics, is my favorite movie of all time and the one I watch when I'm sick or overall need a pick me up. It makes me laugh, it has great fight scenes, Chinese Black magic, and lightning effects that I STILL think hold their own in Hollywood.

Like these, I can offer countless examples and if I ever change my opinion, it's because my tastes have changed or because I see things in a new light, not because someone's opinion was the sole reason for me to sway in regards to how I feel about something. Originally I hated *Mr. Jones* by Counting Crows and now it's a fav song from the 90's along with the fact that they became a band I'm extremely fond of.

By the same token, things I used to love, I've outgrown, like *Mortal Kombat* and *Street Fighter*. It's not that I don't enjoy them at all, but unlike when I was a kid, I'm not as compelled to play or much less purchase a fighting video game simply because other things interest me more. And that's what it's all about, pursuing our interests and exploring what resonates with us throughout our lives, regardless of public opinion.

BE HOW YOU WANT TO BE

Many of us have dreams and aspirations and goals of all types. Maybe we look in the mirror and we want to see a version of us that's more toned, a bit leaner, stronger, has better posture, and looks and feels happier. The questions to answer should be: how to get those changes down and how can you improve yourself with actions rather than wishes?

A lot of people say they want to lose weight. But what they do to go from wishful thinking to an actual state is a very different thing. You can want and wish to be leaner all you want, but if your diet is off, you don't exercise, and you don't take care of yourself, it won't magically happen. The magic in life comes from having a vision and pursuing it. Sure you need that vision, but you also need to have the discipline to do it and that's an essential part of how you define yourself.

Most everything about you is definable by what you put

into it and finding can'ts is easy, but finding examples of people who broke through the can'ts and won'ts to get to the DO abound as well. This book has talked a lot about accountability and choice and the same goes for defining yourself. The more you can own who and how you are, the less you have to worry about keeping up with any acts to impress someone.

Do you want to be calmer? Then meditate, take anger management training, go to a psychiatrist, do Zumba, exercise, eat cleaner, drink more water, cut sugar, cut caffeine, do breathing exercises, whatever... but do SOMETHING. Don't wait for the magic to happen through the laws of attraction because guess what? Those powers often don't work and often leave you waiting. So don't wait. Do. Want to be a successful anything? Then identify what you have to do, hone your skills and go for it. Don't expect life to grant you three wishes plus a bonus one because you donated a dollar with your supermarket purchase. Take active steps to get to where you really want to be in life.

EVOLVING IS GROWING

Some people insist on sticking to their guns and liking something because they have said something was their favorite, so they can't one day simply decide that they stop liking something. Although the sentiment behind this attitude might be pure, it's ill-placed.

Who and how you are at one moment is not the same as who and how you were a year ago and who and how you will be in another year's time. We are in a constant state of evolution so likes and dislikes can and do change with time. Our values can also change with time but those should be a lot more permanent than what we like and this isn't contradictory. Experience defines what we know and what we know determines how we manage life just as much as how we view it. Maybe you're in favor of something until one bit of information causes you to change opinion. This can come from information, a conversation, or the very experience of life.

Trust me, getting pulled over for a DUI or being involved in a car crash because you or someone else was under the influence are merely two very arbitrary examples in regards to opinions about alcohol behind the wheel. A person who is for more freedom to purchase handguns might feel different if someone they know or their child is killed because of a misfire just as much as a person who is completely against guns can change their tune if they're ever held up at gunpoint.

The more we live, the more we learn, and the more material we have to base an opinion on. It's not a bad thing either. It's life. Some values we maintain for life while others are more susceptible to change.

When it comes to behaviors and likes, the dynamic is quite similar. Maybe you're really a yoga enthusiast that needs that first class to find out how much you love it. Maybe trying one particular spice in a dish is the spark you needed to want to pursue cooking as a more meaningful activity and not only a hobby. Maybe a painting class opens you to a whole new world of things you can enjoy, from taking more classes with different techniques and buying art materials to painting along with Bob Ross, traveling to the Louvre and the Prado museums, and keeping an eye out for local art exhibitions.

Life is curious like that for us humans. A passion can be one decision away. A favorite dish is one bite away. A new hobby can be right there waiting for you to try it and discover new pieces of who you are.

But people fear change. What if you don't like something? What if it tastes bad? What if it's boring? What if it's a waste of time? The last question is the one we should focus on the most, but firstly, what if you don't like something? It's not the end of the world. What if something tastes bad? Then you spit it out and have a funny story to tell. What if something is boring? Then you can make fun of it at a later time. Now, what happens if something is a waste of time? Well, that sentiment is down to you and you alone.

Heartbreak is never fun. Being embarrassed sucks. Pain is not something anyone enjoys. But nothing has to be a waste of time unless we deem it so. In my life, I've learned to do my best to enjoy negative experiences and have fun with them, particularly those related to something tasting bad. In regards to pain, I've worked my hardest to get something out of the most negative experiences in my life. There are lessons to be learned and a life to be lived and it's not all going to be fun and games and rose tinted wonders.

I'll offer one example and one of the most important events in my life. When I was 31, I wasn't eating properly, working crazy hours, and pushing my body to the limit in the sense that I would work incessantly, not work out, eat poorly and then expect to surf 4 hours and pay no consequences. One day at a beach in Puerto Rico, my back was tight but I paid no attention to it. I went to say hi to some friends and when I came back to the spot I had been sitting in, I plopped myself on the sand, because after all, it's *sand.*

What happened afterward has been the most intense pain I've ever felt in my life. Landing on my coccyx is something that's happened. It's always an awful experience but on this occasion, it wasn't your typical paralyzing pain... it was worse than that. Something was wrong and the pain only increased. I had gotten a massive back spasm and I couldn't even communicate for 2 minutes. Writhing in pain, no one asked me if I was OK since I probably looked like I was tripping on some illicit substance. The reality is that the pain was so massive and I couldn't move at all to the point that it took me almost a full 3 minutes just to get on my feet. I went and asked for help. They gave me a chair and called some emergency personnel... which took almost two hours to get there, but that's beside the point. I had to call my wife who was an hour and forty-minute drive away from me.

All this gave me a lot of time to think and it was just the

beginning. The drive back was absolutely grueling and every bump felt as if someone was tugging at all the nerves in my lower back. Add to this a 4-hour wait in the ER and you start to get an idea of how fun the whole experience was. When all was said and done, I had a massive back spasm and X-rays showed I have herniated discs in my lower back. I was bedridden a full week and it took me three days just to be able to go to the bathroom unassisted. Walking wasn't the worst part though, it was sitting down and ESPECIALLY standing up. Right after the injury, when my brother and wife went to pick me up, they saw me sitting and didn't think I was that hurt. That was until I tried to get to my feet. From sitting to standing position, it took me almost a full minute and my legs were shaking all the time while tears leaked from my eyes without blinking because of the sheer pain I was experiencing.

That week was a long week. And when you have an overactive imagination, you think... a lot. I thought about where I was in my life, what I was doing, how I was living, and realized that although I enjoyed life, I was more surviving than truly living. I wasn't happy and although I was working on my first novel, I was in more of a standstill than progressing. After that week I decided things needed to change. Exercise needed to be part of my life. I looked for options in care and didn't accept the prognosis of not one but three doctors that suggested varying levels of surgery or medical interventions. I was 31 and I was having none of that, especially since I came in contact with a LOT of information of poor medical outcomes especially for back surgery because of my job.

That's when I truly and deeply decided that I was going to change and change for the better. I was going to improve on who I was every single day and much more than I was already doing. Sure, I'd improved but a lot of old habits were still keeping me from doing what I wanted to do. So I set out a plan and step by step I carried it out, redefining how I lived and how I wanted to feel about the person I was.

It's been seven years since that injury. I've introduced stretching as part of my daily routine. I exercise regularly. I am a little more conscious of what I eat. I have learned dozens of ways to cope with stress to have more options to make sure I'm in the best emotional state as I can even if there are no guarantees. I've had good times and I've had bad times. I've had other painful lessons, but from this lesson through injury, I learned a lot and all it took was one mistake and the decision to learn from that mistake and not settle for surviving.

Every single day I continue to pursue a better version of me. Every day I find new opportunities to be a better version of me. Every day I take steps to the things that drive me. I don't just wish for them, but take active steps towards those goals. Every day I learn to be more honest with myself about a lot of who and how I am. Every day I look in the mirror and say "let's do this." My areas of opportunity might infuriate me, but I know that with discipline and consistency I can achieve anything. This doesn't make me a superhero. This doesn't even make me particularly special. It makes me human in the way that I choose to define it and I can't help but wish the same for you so that you can show us the best humanity has to offer in your own definition of who and how you are.

RETURN OF INVESTMENT

Life isn't meant to be easy, but it is definitely meant to be enjoyed as much as possible. It's not to say that you have to focus solely on the challenges to be had, but it is very possible and it begins by accepting the person you are and learning to love yourself, warts and all. Flaws aren't a bad thing unless you allow them to be. Flaws are an intrinsic part of being human and they are an invitation to grow into the best possible version of us that we can manage to offer. There's plenty of reasons why defining yourself is a good idea, but as with most of the chapters in this book, here's four for you.

1. IT'S EASIER TO LIVE

If you are the only person in charge of defining who you are, that's definitely an easier option than the alternative. Think about all those people you know who need to buy the latest technological wonders, who have to stay up to speed with fashion trends, who watch the movies everyone watches, devour all the shows they're told they have to see, and read only what is trending. Now think of throwing all of that away and focusing on what you want to see, hear, watch, or create. Pandering to others is a way to fake acceptance and appeasing constantly to others is one of the quickest way to misery. If you focus on you, and not obnoxiously so, but sincerely focus on YOU and what YOU like, then you only have to keep track of one set of opinions. Sure, you can share opinions with people and of course you're allowed to be convinced to watch something. There's nothing wrong with any of that. But if you constantly do things to be part of the crowd and be accepted, it's very easy to feel quite empty and as if what you do is never enough. So focus on you. That's hard enough on its own, but wow is it worth your time.

2. YOU WILL ALWAYS KNOW WHAT YOU WANT

Ask someone what they want and they might think they have an idea, but after any degree of introspection, they might realize how little they really know in regards to their goals, dreams, and desires. Quite often we look for comfort and convenience and we forget to seek and actively pursue fulfillment, happiness, and satisfaction. Why settle for quoting the Rolling Stones when you can actively pursue what interests you? I know a lot of people who read books, watch movies, learn languages, and take courses just to impress someone. We've all done it to some degree or another at some point in time in our lives. OK, so what happens after they're impressed? What's left after you've reached that goal? What was in it for you beyond making a good impression? **That** is the danger of not doing things for yourself and instead doing something thinking about someone else and more often than not, you will be shortchanged. If instead you focus on what you're interested in, there's no limit to how much enjoyment you can get from things because you are responding to YOUR interests and YOUR desires. Not anyone else's. Life is a subjective experience whose context we share with other people. But it's ours to enjoy and the more we enjoy on our own terms, the more there will be to enjoy.

3. YOU WILL BE WONDERFULLY UNIQUE

Trends and fads come and go, but who you are remains. So why constantly shift with the tides of fashion and whatever is in vogue? Today's rage can be tomorrow's old news, but if you enjoy something, you don't care about trends. They don't apply to you and it is wonderfully liberating. Not only that, the more you focus on what you like, the more of a unique experience you are able to have. Quirks are particular things that aren't necessarily the norm. It's defined as a peculiarity of action, behavior, or personality; a mannerism. It's a big part of what makes up your personality because it often doesn't fall under any convention, which is a beautiful thing. I am still remembered because of things I did over thirty years ago and everyone has a particular perception of who I am, but a lot of people apparently find something memorable in me. It's not always a good thing, but at the very least, people remember, and if that's my reward for being myself and embracing who and how I am every day, why would I ever even consider stopping?

4. YOUR LIFE WILL BE COMPLETELY YOURS

When you live life on your terms, enjoying the things you like, and following your inner heart compass, your path and journey are exclusively yours. It's a daily adventure and challenge and not something that happens of its own accord. But it's worth every effort you put into living life on your terms. Some people stay at jobs they don't like because it's what they have to do instead of pursuing dreams. They don't take steps towards the things that bring a sense of fulfillment to their life for whatever the reason. Then there are people who work at it bit by bit, eventually getting closer to their dreams. Then there are other people who throw caution to the wind and bet it all on one thing. And there's mid points between these three options. What you have to decide is where you are most comfortable and happy. What place in that spectrum can you honestly say, I'm happy? This is enough. The fact remains that you are the one to decide and define this and no matter the amount of books you read and advice you're given, the life you live is yours and yours alone. The sooner you accept this and take steps to living a life you're happy to live, the better it is for you in the short, medium, and long run. Being clear of how you want to live is not something that comes about in a certain way. Every person has a different epiphany and to varying degrees. But your body is wiser than your brain.

There are some ideas within you that excite you, that make your pulse race, that feel *right*. Listen to your body as well as your brain because your body has perfect hearing and will often guide you when you're not sure which path to take. Will it always be right? Not really. But sometimes taking the wrong path and committing a mistake is part of the path just as much as it is part of the path to make a decision and have everything fall into place. Whatever happens though, accountability and owning your decisions will set you free a lot more than it will hinder your enjoyment of life. So all that remains to be asked is this: what are you waiting to live **your** life?

SUMMARY AND TIPS:

Life is not easy, but it is worth living and enjoying. Defining myself as I see fit has always been a part of my personality and it's allowed me to always be me. Beyond accepting my flaws, I've been able to recognize what I want to improve and why. I've always indulged in trying new things and allowing myself to experience life as fully as I can. That said, my opinions are also my own and they are not blind opinions but informed ones. I'm not saying I'm always right, but if I believe something, it's not merely because I was told I should believe it blindly. I don't believe in blind faith, blind beliefs, or living blindly. That's because blind people have taught me that seeing is a lot more than the simple usage of our sense of sight.

Perception is the way we engage with reality and I choose

to do it on my terms. Are there compromises? Sure. Do I sometimes do things I'd rather not? Of course. It's life, not a joy ride. It is however a ride. It has ups and downs and goes all around. There are sharp corners, big drops, and sometimes the ride breaks down. But it's our ride. Not anyone else's. Your ride is yours, mine is mine, and although we can even share parts of that ride, what you experience is not the same as what I experience... but it's all worth experiencing.

I'm 37 upon completing the first draft of this book. I'm not particularly old, but I'm not young. I'm in that funky midpoint where it's easy to not fit in... and that's how I like to live. Being me enough to be accepted for who I am even though I'm not identical to other people. I enjoy acceptance and praise but will not sacrifice my definition of JD one inch in hopes of gaining more acceptance or praise. I am a Ravenclaw, but I'm more than a Ravenclaw. I am identified as ENFJ but I'm more than that personality type. I was born in August but I'm not just a Leo. I'm me and that me is defined every single day through experiences, interests, and with no agenda except to experience and enjoy the ride we call life.

I could give many tips of how to be more you, but I think it's better if you have that conversation with yourself. You are cooler and more interesting than even you think so already. There are surprises within you waiting to be discovered and that's an amazing thing. The only time limit in regards to discovering yourself and who you are is your lifespan, and even so, there's no guarantee that it's game over once we pass on. There are several theories in regards to what happens when we do, in fact, die. But they're all speculation. All we have for certain is this life and we can't live as if there's any type of guarantee we'll be here tomorrow.

So pull up a chair or go for a walk or anything you want, and have a good conversation with your inner self. Ask what you'd like to do and see what you can do to give it a go. Write down dreams and goals and ideas so you don't forget them. Schedule time to work towards those dreams and aspirations and be more than what people define you as. Remember, life is a ride, your ride, and you can add as many turns and drops as you want, or you can have a kiddy ride with little to no thrills. There's no right answer in regards to what that ride should look like, but it's your ride. So might as well enjoy it.

AFTERWORD

This is my first project ever worked on for NaNo WriMo. If you don't know what NaNo WriMo is, it stands for <u>Na</u>tional <u>No</u>vel <u>Wri</u>ting <u>Mo</u>nth. Now, some people will most certainly contest that this isn't a novel, but no one can say it isn't a book. There's chapters, summaries, an intro, and now this snazzy outro. It's got pages and words and ideas and its first draft was written within a month. Actually, less than a month. I went on vacation and it was a great time with friends and family and for 6 solid days I did not write.

Did I quit? No.

Did I rush? Not so much.

What I did do was be consistent with writing for most of the month and when I had the opportunity to really go for it and write up a storm, I wrote it. It isn't something for everyone but between this and both stints of Camp NaNo WriMo this year, it's been one of the most productive years even with a full itinerary... and there's still a month to go.

I'm sharing this with you because a lot of people do quit during NaNo WriMo and through challenging things in their lives. I'm not saying that's the right or wrong way to do things, but I will say that some people are prone to quit. Others have situations happen in life and the fact of the matter is that situations will often come up. Challenges will arise and you will wonder why it's so easy for other people while it's so hard for you. It happens, but the opposite can happen. You can persevere, you can endure, you can rise beyond the challenges and I highly recommend doing so because some of the best experiences in life will not come easily.

I wrote this book on a whim with nothing but a phrase to start with. From that phrase came the definition of what that phrase means to me and what it can inspire. From there came the idea for a book. From the idea I took several papers and jotted down topics I wanted to discuss. From the topics came subtopics, bullet points, and things I REALLY wanted to touch on if only to put on paper what I hold in my soul.

Peace, love, and maki rolls is something that I've been saying for at least 13 years in my life. It's become kind of a signature and I've never seen anyone say the phrase so this is also my opportunity to own it as fully as I can without paying for copyright. But it is a very *me* thing to say and this was a very *me* book to write. Will it change lives? Who knows? I only know I felt something within me telling me that I should write this. In part because I was in a writing slump and in part because I wanted to show I can write in any genre I choose to, not because of ego, but because I like a good challenge and man do I love writing.

We'll see how the editing process goes but if anything is clear, it's that if you have a goal, the desire to reach it, and the discipline required to reach it, then not even the sky is the limit. So here's to you, and here's to all of us enjoying a little bit of peace, love, and maki rolls.

ABOUT THE AUTHOR

Although JD Estrada now resides in the state of Georgia, home shall always be Puerto Rico. Born, bred, and raised in the Caribbean, any definition of happiness probably includes the ocean in some way or another, which is curious since the closest shoreline to him is at least 4 hours away. Apart from that, he likes to write. As in he REALLY likes to write.

He's written novels, poetry, short stories, essays, and dabbles in as many genres as he can possibly find because he likes a good challenge and likes seeing what is inside him when he looks through new topics, perspectives, and styles. He also writes in English and Spanish because a bilingual nature definitely calls for bilingual artistic expression.

Also an avid bookworm, he can be easily spotted on several social media platforms talking books and doing random things because that's always the most fun. He is very happy to see you've read another one of his books and hopes you are doing brilliantly well.

Acknowledgments:

When it comes to writing thank yous, there's always the risk of forgetting someone. It's not that I'm forgetful as much as there are tons of people I want to thank. That being said, my poetry collections now get short acknowledgment sections and each book will be a case by case thing in regards to how many people I want to thank. On this occasion, there are a LOT of people to thank and I'll do my best to write everyone down. By the way, if you're wondering if this section and others are longer than usual to meet the 50K limit of NaNo WriMo, I have no idea where you got that idea............. :)

To my wife Janelis. You've seen me at my best and worst and have been an essential part of my life for over 13 years. Thank you for the support you've given me and all the ways you take care of me. They are more than I can list and I thank you from the deepest of me for indulging my whackiness and inspiring to keep pushing for greatness. Te amo, Mamomita.

My thanks to you, Mama. Every single day I work hard to make you as proud of me as I am of you. This is another work of love and I know it isn't in Spanish, but I promise more are on their way. I just had to get this one down first. Te amo.

To Juanky and Kibu, I'm proud to call you brothers and every success you have I celebrate. You're both some of the hardest working people I know and offer a great example to others, even your crazy little brother who had the itch to write and scratches it every day. Sheila and Monica, thank you for caring for my brothers, nephews, and your families so much. Being a mother is a full time job and you both work hard at it along with your husbands, which is why my nephews rock so much. Carlos Ignacio, Pablo, Juan Diego, and Marcos. I love you guys and even if I'm in Georgia, I'm always a message, phone call, or text away and always happy to help you guys. Se les quiere and keep living life and enjoying it to the max.

Trobi, my brother from life. How much we've lived and how many surprises and adventures are in store. Here's to you and I'm so blessed to see you walking the walk and showing that if you want to do something, you do it damn it.

Antonio, beyond the music that binds us together, I want you to know how much I love you as a brother. You're an awesome dad and I promise we will create music together. I just need one of these books to hit big. :) In the meantime, keep on rocking in the free world, brother.

To Andrew, my Asian brother from another mother. I hold you in as high esteem as I can and look forward to you conquering those goals, my friend. Regardless of what happens in life, know you are among my favorite people and the Spanish lessons I give you pay off in laughter every time. To success and the smallapotatoes.

To Dad. I miss you and I think about you a lot. I really wish you could have seen some of what I do. In part, because obviously I want you to be proud, but also in part so you see that your influence lives on and that I work hard every day to share the best of you through the best of me.

To José "El Tony" Arocho, although you didn't do this cover, having my artistic trust for a cover is an achievement in and of itself. The relationship we have comes in part from being in tune, in part getting along, and in part trusting each other and giving our best to help the other out. You are a hard working mamma jamma and I'm always sending you and Tania the best wishes. To Tania, keep on conquering new goals and traveling the world so we can get ideas and do the same.

To Cate Evans. Thank you for every single time you've encouraged me to go above and beyond and push harder. Your support to me as a human, a writer, and a friend is priceless. I thank you from the deepest well of me and am proud to see you with all your accomplishments and all those to come. Thank you for being one of the kindest and most generous humans I know who offers an amazing definition of the word "human." To Caitlin Evans, you do your mother proud and I'm always wishing you the best and rooting for all of your future success. To Patricia "Chatty Patty" Buist, thank you for always having time to say hello and wish me the best. Your friendship is one of those lovely surprises you appreciate from life.

To Karen Ohren. We are born into family, but some parts of our life family come along with no blood ties and thousands of miles in between. I know you and yours have had challenging times, but know I'm always here for you and your father. Your mother was always proud on a daily basis because her daughter is not only an amazing human, but a sensational friend. Much love to the Ohrens.

To Larysia Woropay. Your sheer determination and discipline are an example to follow. Taking no for an answer is not in your DNA and I believe in you, your talent, and your work. Keep going forward although I know that's the only way you know where to go to.

To Alex. Overcoming challenges is your daily adventure and me and Jane are always keeping you in our thoughts and hearts. You are as perseverant as they come and we are always rooting for you to find all the happiness that you deserve.

Emily Irizarry, Stacy Rosario, and Aneudy Irizarry, my framily. It's been years since we've met and each and every one of you make me proud. Stacy and Aneudy, your commitment to running and physical events make it clear why wearing Superman attire is beyond adequate in that family. And Emily, you have one of the biggest hearts I know and regardless of the changes life brings your way, know you will always have a frand in me. Mal Ward and Seema Tabassum, two of my favorite poets and friends from around the world. I'm working on both your daydreams and although I do apologize for the delay, I will definitely make the wait worth it. You both inspire with your creative spirits and I'm fortunate to call both of you friends. Even being thousands of miles away, I care a lot for both of you and your families and want you to know that your joy is our joy. May the muses always dance with you and may happiness be in overabundance from England to India and everywhere around.

To Joaquín Rodríguez Kierce. Hard working doesn't even begin to describe you. You're a hell of a guy and you're always at it nonstop. The work you and several people do saves lives and I'm proud to call you friend. That said, we still have that other book to finish ha ha ha. Cheers to you and yours and thanks for always supporting me, brother.

To Eugen and Dinah, here's to having the four Hogwarts houses represented in a magical friendship. I'm happy to see both of you working hard, being successful, growing, and looking to your next adventure. Big may you smile and long may you party.

To Meghan Herrington. My dear Megh, you are the very definition of fighter and I am proud to call you friend. I know you've endured quite the rough patch, but you will come out a stronger and healthier human in the end. May joy continuously find its way to you and may health grant you the peace you so very muchly deserve.

To Madeline Ortiz, your pursuit of your path of enlightenment is beautiful. I am so very happy for you and thank you for always believing in me and always supporting me even when I was just starting out. It means the world and it also fills me with intense joy to see you doing what makes you happy. To Glo Ramírez. Thank you for being such an amazing representation of Puerto Rico in Alaska. Your kind soul and warm smile make the world a better place and your artwork always makes the days better. To Maricel Jiménez. My fellow Puerto Rican indie and the Pixie Momma. I'm loving your books and look forward to more from you in as many ways as possible. Keep aiming for the target and expressing your inner fairy Katniss. Se te quiere conco y agradezco todo tu apoyo continuo.

To Luz "Lulú" María Peña. Seeing you embrace your art is a beautiful thing as well as it is seeing you and your family with so much happiness. My best to the hubs and here's to the art of life and painting our own masterpieces.

To Dianavette Orsini. Your unconditional belief in me encourages me on tough days. I am happy to know you are a teacher so that kids can have a proper educational experience with a top notch human. You always bring you're A-game and I must admit that every con we coincide comes with the guarantee I'll see some epic cosplay and get some soul warming hugs. Cheers and thanks for all the love you always show to me and my dreams.

To Kayra. Time passes by in a flash but the best friendships are all about quality and not quantity. Thank you for always encouraging and supporting me and loving my wife as much as you do. Es fácil quererte and every bit of success you have is cause for celebration.

To Diana Quiett. A friendship 22 years strong and I'm sure we'll be able to meet up so our families can also spend some time together. Thanks for the love and support all these years, for always being there for me even though we're not in touch all the time and for always caring and accepting me with all my kooky madness and all the changes that can happen in 2 decades of friendship.

To Esteban Bird, Papo, I know life brings challenges but you keep going and aiming high. Cheers to you and thanks for always encouraging and being your own brand of awesome.

To My Geekrican family, Zhure, Finees, Rikky, and Edgar. Thanks for all the support all these years and for your enthusiasm in my work. You've always been extra kind to me and I love you guys long time. As for all the amazing and wonderful people I've met at the Puerto Rico Comic Con, thank you for fueling my dreams and supporting my efforts so generously. I'd list all of you, but then this section would be even longer!

To my Indie family: Joe Compton, as kind a soul as you are a hard worker. You always remind why it's always time to Go Indie Now but your example and friendship definitely inspire me to keep going full throttle, brother. To Anaïs Chartschenko, my tea sister and one of my favorite poets (not indie poets, but POETS). Your friendship is a blessing and your support through some of the toughest days I've lived show why you are such a treasure. You make me proud to call you friend and my life is richer for having your words in it. To Christie Stratos, my favorite indie author, your sequel is hot in the TBR and shall be read voraciously soon. Thank you for being such a lovely friend, for sharing your Victorian and chocolate infused passions and for writing amazing stories. To Jason Greensides, now that I'm back to reading, your book will get read and reviewed before the year is over, brother. You rock and I'm always rooting for your continued success so that we may share a beer and some stories. To Joshua Robertson, Lilian Oake, and The Goblin Horde. I love you guys and it shall be in the

232

cards to meet up again to share some laughs, disgusting jelly beans, and coffee. Thanks for being awesome human beans. To CL Cannon, my deepest thanks for your support for Puerto Rico and for having an unwavering commitment to your dream. Cheers to you and much success in all your indie endeavors. To Heidi Angell, synonymous with kindness, you rock and any slice of success and happiness that comes your way is beyond well earned. Always wishing you the absolute best. To Sarah Brentyn AKA the Snark Shark. My fellow Ravenclaw, it's an honor to know you and read you. Your work is as unique as you and just like with your husband, I wish for success to meet up and share a glass of wine and all the stories. To Sunshine Somerville, the wandering indie writer! I'm so happy your moving madness is coming to an end so you can focus on you and the hubs settling down and enjoying life. Look forward to reading you in email or book form because it's always a great thing. To Marnie Cate, here's to embracing your own brand of awesome and writing up a storm. To Papa Dark Realmer, Michael J Elliot. Incredible that such a kind man can have such a dark streak in his writing, but just goes to show that the brightest and kindest hearts can definitely surprise us. Here's to you and all the Dark Realmers. To Amie Irene Winters, one of my fav indie authors with an imagination that is only second to your kindness. I loved reading the entirety of the Strange Luck series and although I know you'll take a break, I do hope the writing bug bites you once again. To AJ Bell, humble strength and a dynamite smile are a testament to a wonderful mother, a great friend, and a great writer. Thank you for the love and friendship and here's to all the inspiration in your stories. To JB Taylor, thanks for always telling things like they are and always wearing your heart on your sleeve. You're awesome, brother. To Theresa Snyder, another tea sister and the dragon momma. You make Farloft proud as much as you delight us readers. Thanks for such generous kindness and for sharing snippets of life with us. Sending all the love to you and your wonderful father, which includes plenty of hugs. To Amanda Armstrong, amazing how time passes and we keep producing great written works (who needs humility, huh? Lol). Thanks for all the laughs, the support, and for raising a wonderful princess. Know your pride for Mia is appreciated as is your friendship. To Amanda Mabry, a generous soul, a kooky lass, a talented and honest writer, and a dynamite human. From your adventures in the pink kayak, to that Colgate smile, it's a pleasure to call you friend and to be able to count on you for anything. Always happy to support talented people with hearts of gold. To Rebekah Jonesy, hilarious, genuine, and kind AF. That's you in a nutshell but your support for Puerto Rico during this time of need has been a beautiful thing to enjoy. Thank you for all the love and support and my thanks to your hubby for his service as well. May you help us find all the definitions of love. To Myk Pilgrim, my friend, may your wand ever be springy, may your writing ever be flowing, and may your asshole editor release a book of his own. You are all sorts of awesome and one day we shall share beer, shots, and a concert, because we shall make it so!

To Annalyn Díaz and Vivian Acevedo, it's a gift to be able to meet online friends who support my work in real life. Meeting you guys has been a huge highlight and your continued support goes a long way to fueling the fire of a Puerto Rican author. Se les quiere mucho.

Sarah Loken, your support at such hard times in my life means the world. I'm always rooting for you and your happiness. May the Goddess bring you joy, good tidings, and peace of mind. Stephen Cleath, one of the kindest guys I know. Keep writing and push for your dreams. The world needs more dreamers and you're a wonderful one. Amy Dionne, the Pagacorn. Such support, such kindness through thick and thin, thanks for always being there and listening to a scruffy guy out when he needed it. You rawk and the goddess works through you so keep on keeping on. To Nadia "NadiPops" Fortuna, to have the support of someone who reads so incessantly means I'm doing something right. To have the friendship of someone as awesome as you confirms it as well. Thanks for always having a kind word to say about me and the words I share. To Sandy V, for in depth reviews and in depth kindness. Your reviews are honestly a source of inspiration and I thank you for all the support. To Tracie Behmlander, thanks for the unconditional support and kindness. I can count on you for a nice thing to say in all the random things I share. Thanks for that and much more. To Richard Gibney, you are a wonderful loon with a heart the size of the moon, so cheers to you, your support, and your wonderful words. I've pending to read you and will get to that sooner than you think. To Asghar Abbas, you are proof that words can bring people together from around the world my friend. Cheers to you and I will be reading a lot more of you soon. That said, thanks for always supporting me and my crazy adventures. To Barbara Elin, so kind and generous, thank you for proofreading another non-fiction book I wrote and for always supporting so wonderfully. Counting on good friends helps one keep pushing and you are an awesome friend at that. The UK tour is a must and we shall share tea and stories a plenty. To Katya Lipnitskaya, my dancing friend, here's to the muses that brought us together. Thanks for always being there and for always pushing to show the best light within you. To Claudette, my Draem compatriot. It's always fun to catch up and see what manic and wild ideas are going on with you. Always sending the best wishes your way because it's easy to do with good people. To Kevin Corvus, my Island braddah, we shall share beers and waves and that's one of the main goals of making it as a writer, my friend. May Fridays always bring metal and the cold beer be ever chilled. To Eric Syrdal, a remarkable poet only surpassed by his qualities as a human. You rock my friend so may your quill be ever inked to allow us to bask in your words. Shannon Adams, one of the coolest gingers I know and a friend who not only supports me and my quirkiness, but always has a friendly word to share. You've been there through thick and thin and I thank you for all that support. Quentin Zach Cooper, AKA The Walking Casino. My friend, thank you for all your belief in me and your generosity towards me, my loved ones, and my Island. You're a good friend and I look forward to more videos of you cooking up a storm. Cheers, brother. To Ayla, the yogi poet. A kind friend who is always there to offer support. Your infectious joy is as treasured as your kind spirit. Thanks for everything. Jennifer Newman, sock royalty if there ever was one. I'm so happy you won one of my book giveaways and I'm beyond happy to have you as a main part of the Sock Family. Cheers to you and your never ending cheer. To Liz Lebrón, your work in support of Puerto Rico inspires to keep going and doing all we can to help our brothers and sisters on the Island. Also very happy that you were one of the winners of the #humans4PuertoRico giveaway. Your labor is commendable as is your commitment to helping others. To Roger Jackson, my prose bro. It's great to see you in a better state and sharing your awesomeness. Now give us some more of them lovely words. To Hope Denney, always wishing you and yours well even with all the challenges you've faced. May plenty of health come your way to keep sharing your wonderful words. To Anna Maria Rochelle, my Georgian sister. So many dreams and enough enthusiasm, strength, and energy to go for each and every one of them. You're awesome and I'm proud to call you friend, my ginger sister. To Veronica Brannon, your commitment to fitness definitely inspires me to keep in shape and stay healthy and that there are no goals that can't be reached if you have discipline and heart. To Pat Sherard, you've always been especially kind to me and believed in me and my work. From novels to sock posts, you're always there rooting and that means the world to me. To Bianca Bowers, a friend from down under who has a wonderful soul and great words to share. Here's to all the fun between friends and for encouraging Rich to keep the crazy going. To Faith Lane, thank you for showing that beliefs need not divide us. You're a true friend and I wish you all the success. To Sonangely Colón, for unconditional support all these years, sock gifts, and all the hugs we owe each other. Thanks for always having a smile handy to share. To Robin Lincecum, my favorite Louisianan. Thanks for having offered me so much support the last 13 years. It's great to have your friendship and I'm always wishing you the absolute best for you and your family. To Reedabee, another wonderfully quirky friend. You always bring a smile and are as unique as you are kind. Keep on rocking your awesome self. To May Davenport, thanks for the IG support and for always having a kind word to share. Cheers to you and yours and may coffee always be there to keep you company.

To Myrth Lim, an idol if there ever was one. Here's to

wonderful people who give their best no matter what life brings their way. To Katie Utke & Kyle Kubitz, may the ghosts dance with you as you show how much we still have to learn from life and the afterlife. To Mafalda Lopes, it's amazing the wonderful random people we meet in life and how they are so giving in regards to support and kindness. To Kate Anne Everward, for genuine friendship across the world. I wish you and your family safety and happiness. To Sage, you're a wonderful friend and our friendship has taught me so much. Here's to shared music, words, life lessons, and friendship. To Jesse Avilés, for pushing me to get better at what I do, whether in written form or on my video channel. To Francisco Muñiz, my fellow author. Proud to call you friend and a pleasure to read you. To Clarence C, gender doesn't define friendship and I thank you for always pushing to keep Puerto Rico in the minds of many and for supporting wonderful causes. To Rose Weed, your success is our success and I am always rooting for you. To Linda Evans, for indulging in my whacky shenanigans and always offering support. To Lori Carnegie Ryan, for poetic inspiration, kindness, and unconditional friendship. To James Lovette Black, thank you for always pushing for what's right and cutting through the BS. Also thanks for answering complicated questions with such patience. To Coral Bennet, thank you for offering so much support and reading all my work. That means the world to me and I'm fortunate to have you in my corner. To Michelle C, thank you for gifting me the Little Prince AND your friendship.

From casual cosplay to being all sorts of awesome, I'm thankful for knowing you and am always wishing you and yours all the joy. To Ellie McInerney, few people go for it like you do and you are a kind and wonderful inspiration to take no crap, dare to dream, and release the inner badass. To Tosha Michelle, from interviewing me to the adventures of Tucker, it's always a cool thing to be in touch. To Jack Cheng, the man, the myth, the legend! Cheers to you for going for it, brother. Your example inspires to keep going and pushing for those dreams be them here or somewhere in the cosmos.

A special thanks to Nintendo and the creators of Super Mario, The Legend of Zelda, the creators of Final Fantasy, Metroid, Metal Gear, Secret of Mana, Xenogears/Xenoblade, Chrono Trigger, Journey, Flower, Little Big Planet, and all the amazing games that have enriched my life. To experience a playable story is something I wish upon each and every person to expand their horizons at the same time as they tap into an unknown part of their soul.

To my BookTube peeps, what a curious way of making friends, but what an amazing lineup. Amarinske, my Dutch friend, thank you for all the support and enthusiasm as well as kooky videos from your country. Here's to focusing on your dreams, writing up a storm, and sharing more festival adventures with us. To Sage, thank you for teaching me so much about life and so many things I had no idea of.

It's awesome to call you friend and here's to this new chapter in your life. To Olivia, one of my absolute favorite booktubers. You rock not because you have a cool BookTube channel, but because *you* rock. Cheers to being genuine, kind, supportive, and super talented. To Ola Quinn, my lovely friend, thank you for your unconditional support and some of the reviews that most inspire me to keep pushing for excellence. You rock and I'm so happy you're embracing your passions so much. Cheers and keep being awesome even if it is your default setting. Ben Sanders, damn do I need to read your book. Thank you so much for the support and for that push to do the Hurricane Maria Tag. At a moment when I was broken, you showed that a kind word can help us do what we have to do. Brittany Moore, my lovely author friend, I'm so proud for you publishing your first book. Cheers to you and here's to the words that bring us creative types together. To Brittany Reads, it's amazing that I don't know your last name, but such is life in the interwebs. Thank you so much for reading and reviewing my work and for having one of the most fascinating channels out there. Sending you and your family all the best wishes and so happy to know you and call you friend. To Emily Cait, my first buddy read!!! Boy that was great and it was fascinating to compare notes so in depth about American Gods. Cheers to you and much success in all your endeavors. To Britt, more genuine people aren't common so cheers to being you and rocking you. It's always great to be in touch and wishing you all the best in all your adventures. To Amanda Laurell, who would have thought someone so cheeky and funny could have such a big heart. May the wine gods always keep your glass full and may your TBR be ever spicy, curious, and fascinating. Thank you for all the support with the Hurricane Maria Tag and just for being awesome. To Courtney Pickles, with a sock collection as awesome as your book collection, it's always awesome to compare notes and chat it up. Cheers to you and thanks for always being such a great sport with tags, sock it to me madness and any kookiness. To Lauren McCormick, I am so, so happy you won the grand prize for the #humans4PuertoRico Giveaway. Hope you enjoyed the package and look forward to your thoughts. Thanks for all the love and support and here's to a very booktastic year. To Shelby Fox, as sweet and kind as it gets. Thanks for all the support throughout our booktube adventures. Always rooting for you and your goals, so may the beer be cool, the coffee be strong, and the wine be delicious in all your adventures in life. To Travis West, thanks for all the booktube and book support. Rooting for you to not only find the best coffee in the world, but to write up a storm, my friend. To Nash and Xiomy, it's friggin awesome to meet such awesome Puerto Ricans through something as random as BookTube. Cheers to you and my best to you and yours. To Jessi "Rebel Reads" Trafton. Thanks for always being a good sport with the sock madness and for being such a genuine friend. You are awesome and I'll be reading Badger Clark quite soon. To

Alina Popescu, fellow indie author and overall awesome person. Wishing you much success with the writing and that whatever you get to read doesn't inspire the fires of hell! To Kelsey, thank you for all the support during the aftermath of Hurricane Maria with Puerto Rico, it means a lot and I'm wishing you the best always. To William the Baldbook Geek, my friend, thanks for always bringing all sorts of dapper to SockItToMe and for always being honest to the core. To Jaydee Archer, my science loving friend, we shall share that sushi and plenty of life adventures, hopefully including a sumo tournament :D To Camille Dent, another ultra-kind booktuber with a heart of gold. Thanks for your individual efforts to help the people of PR. You're awesome and if you ever need a reminder, let me know. To Kim Barboo, it rarely gets kinder than you. Thank you for the love and support through such hard time and for genuinely helping and coming from a kind place to help me and mine. You are so awesome and I look forward to all your success in as many fields as you choose to tackle. To Anne from Book Your Imagination, kindest thanks for such fascinating life, book, reading, and quirky insights. To Michael S. Deutsch, here's to health, happiness, and always keeping it real like you always do.

To Catalina Cobián, my wonderful sister. Se te quiere conco and it's so wonderful to have you nearby to snag a hug from time to time to show that family isn't just genetics. Thanks also to your other half, Carlos Sánchez, for being outrageous with what he says but as genuine as it comes to who he is. To Génesis Caro, Syndey Ramírez, Mónica Palacios, and so many other kind souls who have connected through the Puerto Rico Comic Con, my life is richer by knowing people as cool as you and to know you enjoy what I create means the world. To Wanda Rivera, Titi Ruth, Alyssa Calimano, Cristina Herrera, Vivianette Cintrón, Ivonne Acevedo, Cristina Riefkohl, Myriam Aguilú, Vivian Arthur, Maité Negrón, Sharon Huertas, Mariela Rodríguez, Mercy Acevedo, Victor de León, Sylnés Centeno, and everyone else at MMM. We worked together for years and your support in different parts of my journey was instrumental in reaching where I have and will continue to reach for. My heartfelt thanks.

To my PM family, Ricky, Rosa, Priscilla, Freddy, Víctor, Hernán, Adrián, Edwin, Rocío, Perla, Ale, Sofía, Lorena, Andrea, Aurora, Salvador, Rodrigo, Rodolfo, Maureen, Eduardo, Patty, Liliana, Caio, Jeffrey, Ava, Samir, Ben, Omar. It takes a special group of people to help me cope with the distance from home and the beach. You guys make every day a fun adventure so that work doesn't feel that much like work. Thank you for not only supporting me, but going along with banana themed wackiness. You guys rock and here's to having a great time every day.

To Anna Dunn, thank you for sharing your traveling adventures and writing ordeals. You inspire as much as you share slices of the world. To Kelly "Sir Rainbow Skychild" Damon, damn you're talented! Keep rocking it and I look forward to reading each other's work and listening to each other's music to compare notes. To Amber Eats books, such a sweet friend. Thanks for all the love and support and answering the dozens of tags! Wishing you a wonderful readtastic year and the best wishes always. To Karen Runwright, my Caribbean Sister, may your writing be as evocative as the wonderful books you read. You are a delight and thank you for always asking about my family and the Island. To Peter Clark, my favorite booktuber will most likely be one of my fav writers, I suspect. So here's to finishing your novel and sharing it with the world along with all your awesomeness. Although I'm sure I'm forgetting someone, this list is mental enough as it is so let's go to the next category, shall we?

My thanks to Chris Cornell, Prince, Lemmy, Scott Weiland, Angus Young, Tom Petty, Shannon Hoon, Layne Staley, Kurt Cobain, and David Bowie, among many others who are no longer with us. Your legacies continue to inspire and I shall forever cherish your music. To Pearl Jam, Elbow, Radiohead, Soundgarden, Blind Melon, Nine Inch Nails, Tool, Tori Amos, Ani Di Franco, AC/DC, The Eels, Days of the New, Alice in Chains, Pink Floyd and countless others, thank you for sneaking your way into my work. I love your cameos.

To my Sock Family, it's awesome to be able to finish this book and win at NaNo WriMo on a Sock it to me day. It's good silly fun we share, but it brings a lot of joy to see people indulging in a little silliness.

To Neil Gaiman, Frank Herbert, Douglas Adams, JK Rowling, Terry Pratchett, CS Lewis, and JRR Tolkien, your worlds of words make my life richer and I can only hope that people enjoy my work a fraction of what I enjoy yours.

And finally, to Terence D'Acosta, my brother from Nepal. We've known each other for over ten years and we had lost touch, but life is random in the way that it brings friends back together. Some people find each other through random circumstances, but only we were able to reconnect thanks to the magic of a little peace, love, and maki rolls. Wishing you and yours and your country peace and the absolute best today and every single day. Godbless, brother.

HUMANS 4 HUMANS

If you follow me on social media, you'll might have seen my #Humans4PuertoRico efforts. Those efforts continue because my home needs a lot of help and month by month I evaluate the causes that are helping in the Island as well as small businesses to support in any way I can.

That said, #humans4PuertoRico was not an effort limited to Puerto Rico. Donations have been encouraged for hurricane victims in Houston, Florida, the Caribbean, the USVI, and Puerto Rico. Support has also been called for people affected by the Spain, Canada, Oregon, and California wildfires as well as survivors of the earthquake in Mexico and survivors of all the terrorist shootings that happened in 2017 alone. That's because this is all part of efforts I shall be carrying on from now on under the **Humans 4 Humans** moniker. What this will entail shall evolve as new needs keep surfacing. The idea is to inspire people to offer Thoughts and Action, to be a part of the solution, to not limit themselves to simply wish to help, but actually do so.

We live in a time where we have all the resources to be active participants in relief efforts and apart from that, we are all human and plenty of people around us need help. So this is a call to action to give the best we have to offer. To not wonder, but do. To give and give freely and not limit ourselves to what is left over. These are turbulent times and I am a firm believer that we should not only stick together, but help as many people as we can in whatever way we can. Sometimes raising awareness is enough, sometimes a hug is all that is needed, but my wish is to find as many opportunities to help and listen to that voice within that says *help your fellow human.*

I do not believe in racism based on age, gender, sexual

preference, creed, social class, income, or health status. I believe in dialogue. I believe that although bad things happen, we can also bring forth good things to maintain the balance. How can we do it? That's a great question, and I hope each and every one of us work tirelessly to find as many answers to that question as possible.

As part of these efforts, I shall continue to offer what I can to help others. If you have a classroom of students that you think could benefit from a chat with me, please contact me. If you see me at a convention and want to write but have questions, ask. I shall always work hard to make time. If you have a cause you believe in and think my support could help, by all means, ask. Many people have asked and many people I've been able to help. But it took someone to ask and offer me the opportunity to help. My thanks for your support, for reading me, for your kindness, and for giving me the opportunity to help. My best to you, and as always... Peace, love, and maki rolls.

Also by JD Estrada

Novels:

Only Human

Shadow of a Human

(Books 1 and 2 of the Human Cycle)

Poetry:
Between the Tides:
Ebbs of poetry in a stream of thought

Dark Strands:
Stirrings beneath the surface

Captured Moments:
Glimpses of life caught in verse

Pensando en Metáforas

Black Tie Affair

Roulette of Rhymes

Short story collections:
Daydreams on the Sherbet Shore Vol. 1

Bilingual Works:
Twenty Veinte

Non-fiction
For Writing Out Loud

Social Media Goodness

Blog

www.jdestradawriter.blogspot.com

Twitter / Instagram / Google +/
YouTube / Facebook

@JDEstradawriter

A final request

Firstly, my kindest thanks to you for reading my work. It means a lot and if it's not too much trouble, I would wish to ask one final request, a favor if you will.

Regardless of whether you enjoyed this book or not, I'd love if you could take a moment and rate this work and any other you've read on Amazon, Barnes & Noble, and/or Goodreads. You see, being an indie author means I don't pay for ads and that my work gets to other people based on reviews and referrals. It is by far the hardest thing to receive as a writer but actually something that helps massively.

So good or bad, let your opinion be known. Tell others of my work and of any other indie person because on social media in general, authors who don't need the buzz, who already have a marketing team get talked about extensively. But us indie authors? We depend on people like you. So if it's not too much to ask, a review would go a long way to helping each of us and give further wings to our future works.

My thanks to you and til next we meet in worlds of words.

JD

Made in the USA
Columbia, SC
23 May 2018